# IRISH CRIMINAL

## THE TRUE STORY OF BRENDAN QUINN

### WRITTEN BY STEVE WRAITH

**Mojo Risin'**
*Publishing Ltd*

Published in 2020 by Mojo Risin' Publishing Ltd
www.mojorisinpublishing.com

British Library Cataloguing in Publication Data:
A catalogue record for this book is available from
the British Library

ISBN-13:
978-1-9163867-4-7

Cover design
David Stanyer

Layout
Neil Jackson, Media Arts
www.media-arts.co.uk

Printed & bound by PrintGuy
Proudly published Up North

# Preface

I would like to take this opportunity to say a special thanks to the people who helped and encouraged me to have this book written.

My parents who I love more and more each day. My daughter Lauren who made me a proud Grandfather. To true friends in West Belfast, health and happiness.

To my long term ex Tracey, you were always special and a good friend.

Friends in Armagh, Dublin, and England, you all know who you are.

To my son, you are the nicest fella I have ever met.

To Steve Wraith and his friend in the same town, thanks.

Life's a long road and it's good to have decent friends.

*Brendan Quinn, October 2020.*


I would like to thank Brendan for the opportunity to put his story onto paper and thank Neil Jackson and Dave Beaney for their help and support putting this book together.

*Steve Wraith, October 2020.*

# Chapter One: De Geerhorst

With a hood over his head and his hands cuffed behind his back, the prisoner was pulled roughly out of the armoured Mercedes and led into high risk prison, De Geerhorst in Sittard. The escort consisted of about twenty armed members of the BOT, a special assistance unit of the Dutch Ministry of Justice. These units are used during the transportation of maximum risk prisoners.

It was the 30th of August 1991 and this particular prisoner was destined for the Extra Beveiligde Inrichting (EBI), a special secured unit of this jail. Holland had four of these EBI's now, meant for the 48 heaviest prisoners in the country. As well as Sittard (in the south of the Netherlands) there were EBI's in Leeuwarden (north), Rotterdam (west) and Hoogeveen (north east).

These special wings had only been around for about a year and a half and were meant to end the series of escapes that had plagued Holland in recent years. Each EBI – a prison within a prison – housed eight maximum security prisoners in two completely separated isolation units of four maximum security prisoners each. This unit consisted of the Turk Husnu A., the Dutch Belgian Jozef 'Joe' de M, the Colombian Ruben Londoño and Brendan Quinn from Dublin, Ireland.

At 28 years old Quinn was reputed to be a 'very violent maximum security prisoner'. He had already escaped from Pentonville prison in North London and was charged with two armed robberies and a tram-hijacking in Amsterdam. His life had consisted of escaping, robbing, kidnapping, being behind bars and escaping again.

He sought his fortune in banknotes, preferably sports bags full of them. It didn't guarantee a comfortable life. On the contrary, there was never any peace, always on the run and armed to the teeth. His intention had been to lie low in Holland. It had all gone – to use an understatement – quite differently.

The prisoners on the unit seemed like decent people. Husnu was forty years old and sentenced to fourteen years because of the possession of ninety kilos of heroine. He had a great sense of humour and was also as sharp as a razor. Joe the Belgian guy had to do eleven years after a series of armed robberies. He was just a very polite man. Londoño was the most interesting person of this company. Like Husnu he was forty. Londoño was a very intelligent man and grasped things easily, despite speaking only moderate English.

The Colombian was doing 16 years for cocaine smuggling. This huge capture had led to a national scandal, the so called IRT affair. In this affair, a parliamentary investigation committee was set up to check the infiltration techniques of the special police unit, IRT.

On February 28th 1990 Londoño was caught red-handed in a shed in the harbour of IJmuiden with a batch of 2,658 kilos of Colombian coke. The lot, hidden in barrels of frozen fruit juice, had a purity of 98% and a street value of more than a €1.2 million. An amount of this size had never been caught before in a European country. Holland was stunned.

Londoño had been even more surprised, but for another reason. According to him the freight didn't involve 2,658 but 3,500 kilos. As he was carried away with four fellow Colombians, 800 kilos vanished without a trace.

Londoño told Brendan that originally there were 4,500 kilos of pure coke stored in the 'European distribution centre' in IJmuiden. The stuff was from different Colombian drugs exporters and destined for dozens of buyers all over Europe. From these 4,500 kilos, 1,000 kilos had already been sold, so that left the 3,500 kilos that was found.

An engineer, Ruben Dario Garzon Londoño was described as a captain of industry of the Colombian American Medellin cartel. For that reason, the Dutch intelligence services were quite afraid. They knew that the tentacles of the cartel would reach to the farthest corners of the world. The long arm of the South-American drug mafia would surely try to liberate Londoño.

Shortly after his arrest the police station of the city of Haarlem was transformed into a fortress, guarded with armoured vehicles and special forces. During the court hearing the toughest security measures in Dutch history were used. Commando troops were standby. Judges and the public prosecutor wore bullet-proof vests under their gowns.

The amount of drugs was so huge the mayor of Haarlem started an investigation into whether or not the civilians in the area of the incinerator in North-Amsterdam would get stoned when the white powder was destroyed.

From his cell, Londoño wrote a paper campaigning for the legalisation of drugs, titled 'Social-juridicial perspective of drugs'.

The unit was a specially built jail within the grounds of another jail with its own staff and rules. It was like a very secure Big Brother show. Every move was being watched by cameras and staff. At the same time, Brendan watched every move of the screws. Every single detail could be of importance in planning a way out. He had to get out of there, one way or another.

The cells were equipped with a bed, table, chair, television, sink and toilet. The windows were roller bars with wire behind them. The view from the cell was of a gravel path around a mound of grass where the regular prisoners were able to walk and exercise.

Stepping out of the cell there was a small corridor. To the left there was a glass office where the screws sat watching, above them there was a camera also watching. To the right was the way out of the unit. Two heavy steel doors closed it off, and in between the doors was a metal detector frame. One door wouldn't open until the other had closed. The screws would ask for the locked door to open only when the prisoners had walked through the detector.

In the corridor were five cells; four cells for Brendan and his other inmates and one for the stores. Opposite the cells there was the screw's kitchen and shower room. Life in the unit revolved around this little place.

The daily routine for Brendan and the other inmates of this prison withn a prison began at 8.30 a.m, when the cells were unlocked for work. This didn't mean much more than sitting at a table in a large room at the end of the corridor, putting plastic clips together for an electric plug. After an hour they were then locked up until mid-day. The door was only opened for a meal to be delivered, which was pushed to the door on a trolley.

At 2.30 p.m. the door was unlocked for one hours air in the yard. This yard consisted of a patch of grass in the middle with a dirt track around it. Tall walls completely squared off the yard with two rolls of razor wire at the top. The yard was fully covered by CCTV cameras. There was no single blind spot. Four guards stood in the yard while prisoners exercised, others watched from an office and of course via the cameras as well.

After their break for air Brendan and his fellow prisoners were unlocked until 8.30 p.m. This allowed them to cook a meal or shower or just talk amongst themselves. Every word was monitored and taped by listening devices.

On Thursday evenings they were allowed to use the gym, which was located at the end of the left corridor of unit. Each time EBI prisoners were moving the whole of the prison was locked down first. This was annoying for everyone involved. Sittard EBI were very paranoid about security.

The gym room was small. It contained weights, bikes and an exercise machine. There were four regular screws and two sports instructor screws that stayed continuously while the four prisoners were in there. Two windows looked onto the yard, where they exercised in the afternoons.

The screws in the unit were extremely arrogant and self-assured. The animosity between the screws and prisoners was openly evident and barely contained.

Brendan and his fellow prisoners got on quite well, although no-one trusted one another. He would often smile at this at night in his cell. He didn't trust anybody and only he knew he was not staying in jail. He had to go it alone. However, with the situation he was in, that was a big problem. The unit was brand new and built like a safe. No expense was spared on security. It would be hard to escape from.

As the days came and went, Brendan would watch the other three prisoners, sussing them out, making his mind up about them. He felt that Husnu and the Colombian would go if they could, but Joe wouldn't. Joe made clear that he was fighting his appeal and didn't want to put his chances at stake by attempting to escape.

Joe made Brendan laugh many times. He dressed in suits and ties on the unit, while Ruben, Husnu and Brendan mostly wore shorts, t-shirts and trainers. Joe was a very sociable guy with a warm personality. There's an Italian saying, which roughly translates as: 'Jail time cuts in half in good company'. Anyone who has spent years in jail will agree with that.

Still though, Brendan did not trust them fully. It would be much too dangerous to cooperate with any of them. It was bad enough being in this unit without telling the wrong person what was occurring.

Brendan had noticed a steel plate above the shower and just below the ceiling. It had six steel screws, which could be removed. As the shower was the only place on the unit which was out of sight of the cameras he thought it was worthwhile seeing if the security wing had a way out.

He waited until one of the other inmates was cooking dinner in the small kitchen and went for a shower. It so happened that during the cooking he could take a knife without anyone noticing it. With this knife and a small nail clipper he fumbled at the screws but he only had a short window of time. This experiment would need several attempts as after each meal had been cooked the small kitchen was inspected thoroughly. All cooking utensils were counted so before the meal was finished, the knife had to be back in the kitchen.

After a few weeks of this routine Brendan had managed to take off the steel plate. Behind the plywood on which it was screwed down, there was a big, round aluminium air vent. Eventually he managed to squash this vent to see what was behind it. It mirrored the inside: plywood, then steel. It led into the yard where they exercised.

During exercise he observed where it led out onto the yard. The cameras covered it and it was lit up with spotlights. If he could crawl through this vent from the shower to the exercise yard, he would have to race against the clock. Everything would depend on how fast he could get over the rolls of razor wire at the top of the surrounding walls. If this worked, he would be out of the unit, but still inside the main jail!

Brendan knew he would need outside help on the actual escape. Guns, cars, routes and safe houses. It would take months to sort all the details out, especially as communication was difficult with the visits watched extremely closely and bugged. As the weeks turned into months though, the escape plan was looking very feasible. The communication with the outside world was as solid as it could be in this situation. Prospects became even better when a screw suddenly handed his services on a silver platter, after a small disagreement. The screw had insulted Husnu so heavily about his Turkish origin Brendan had gone for him in the workshop and shoved his head between the bench-vice. 'And now you are going to make some apologies to Husnu' he commanded. Turning his head to Husnu Brendan shouted: 'Should I crack his head, Husnu?' The Turk was scared stiff. With his hands rubbing his painful head the screw wriggled himself out of the bench-vice. 'You're not finished with me', Brendan told him. 'You bet I will pay you a visit as soon as I'm out of here. I will kill you'.

A few days later on the excercise yard the very same screw made an approach. 'Brendan, I had a look on your files to see what kind of figure you are and I've seen that you escaped from London. For the right price I can help you to escape again. I can provide you with weapons and I know you can provide me with money'.

I didn't trust this guy an inch. He was one of these screws who was after

6

Londoño's money. They knew he was immensely rich and hovered round him like slavering dogs, trying to make a deal with him. To test this screw, Brendan gave him an assignment. He had to smuggle a sealed and coded letter to a car park. The receiver would read the letter and burn it immediately afterwards.

The first time the bent screw brought a letter, he was forced to get into a car and brought to a safe house. There he was stripped naked and checked for bugs. As he turned out to be clean, Brendan's contacts showed him the money and a revolver and he was told: 'If you take the money, keep to the deal or go the other road!'. The screw chose to take the money.

Despite the worry of a double cross, he kept his part of the deal and Brendan now had a good way to speak with the outside. The way the coded letters read, it was looking like he could get out of this EBI around Christmas 1992.

# Chapter Two: Choppers, Weapons and Ladders

Ruben wasn't himself, he seemed to be up to something. It wasn't long before Brendan's feelings about him were proved right and Ruben approached him with a proposition. 'I have a helicopter coming. During our exercise period we'll be picked up. How about it? Are you in?'

Of course he was, he didn't have to think about it! Ruben went on: 'Before the rope ladder is dropped down from the chopper, a semi automatic weapon will be dropped into the yard, wrapped in a folded towel to cushion the fall. You'll need to get this and keep the screws away until we're in the chopper'. Brendan had no problems with this. They didn't want any mistakes and sometimes a gun is the only way to prevent mistakes. Actions speak louder than words, as they say.

It wouldn't be Ruben's first attempt to escape. In the months before he was involved in a couple of tries. In June 1991 he was the driving force behind an attempt with a few prisoners from the EBI-unit of prison De Schie in Rotterdam. The mission failed. Shortly after that a group of liberators tried to get him out of the prison in Arnhem, close to the German border. Using collapsible aluminium ladders, they climbed over the prison wall and approached Ruben's cell. They used a cutting torch to remove the bars, but ran out of time and had to leave the same way they came in.

The two men were waiting every day for the chopper to arrive, while out on excercise. Ruben wouldn't reveal the day, which Brendan found a little odd but if he'd been in his shoes he probably would have done the same. They kept up this routine for days. The days had turned to weeks, when one day a chopper flew low into the prison. This was the moment but Londoño looked anxious. Slightly hesitating they shuffled to the centre of the exercise yard. Then, as the chopper flew closer, the word 'POLICE' on the body became clear. Quickly the lads started jogging again, hoping they didn't give anything away by their reation to the helicopter. That night, while lying on the bed in his cell Brendan began to wonder if Ruben's chopper was coming or not. In prison you tend to worry about details on situations you can't control, as there's not much else to do.

Early next morning, the door to his cell was opened. 'Quinn!', a screw shouted. 'You're in court today. You've got to be ready for transport in twenty minutes.' The special assistance team BOT, arrived soon after and led him to one of the three armoured cars. Mostly they used three Mercedes. The lead and the rear had a driver and a passenger aboard. The other four armed agents went in the middle car with the prisoner. The BOT-members were equipped with handguns (Walther P5) and machine guns (Heckler & Koch).

A black hood was put over his head, hands cuffed behind his back and thrown into the back between two agents. They never spoke more than a couple of words. Mostly they used hand signals and Brendan could hear the sounds of

rubbing and snapping fingers. Sometimes on these transports it wasn't unheard of to have the odd 'friendly' voice whispering through the hood: 'The first bullet is for you if someone stops the car!'
Brendan never bothered responding to these comments and today he was only focused on leaving the jail and Holland.

After arriving at the court building he was placed in the cells below the courthouse. As he waited there the door was opened and another prisoner was pushed in. He was dressed in designer clothes and had a thick gold chain and watch. The two men exchanged a polite hello and Brendan laid back down on the bench. The other man walked up and down a couple of times, pacing, and wiped the wooden bench opposite before sitting on it.

For a couple of minutes the two men sat in silence. Eventually the other prisoner said: 'You're not the friendliest of guys, are you?'
Brendan smiled and replied: 'Sometimes.'
'Where is your accent from?' he asked.
'It's Irish'.
Brendan watched cautiously as the other man got up, came over and whispered in his ear: 'Is your name Brendan Quinn?'
After a confirmatory nod from Brendan the man went on:
'That means that you are in Sittard EBI with a Colombian guy'.
'That's right'.
Then holding Brendan's arm he gave him a piercing look and said 'Tell the Colombian I'm his pilot and I'm doing two years!'
Brendan couldn't believe his ears. In one second, every fragment of hope he had on an escape by helicopter was gone. Clearing his throat he told the man: 'Fine, I'll pass the message on'.

Back in Sittard that night he told Londoño what was said. He was visibly stunned and he ranted quietly about the pilot in perfect Spanish, and broken English. Eventually agreeing to forget it for now Brendan then revealed his own plans to break out. That certainly cheered Londoño up.

In the coming days the lads decided never to discuss the full topic in one place or on one day. The microphones would pick up everything on tape. They talked about their plans in the yard while jogging and in the gym. This way they could arrange everything. The main problem was getting over the two walls. If they could get onto the first wall by themselves, they could whistle for someone waiting to throw a rope over with a gun attached. By then they'd be on top with the screws and police on the way.

After a lot of observing and discussing, they both came to the decision that if people could come into the prison and over the next wall into the unit, they could pass a gun through the window and leave straight away. Then the two escapees could just take care of the screws and follow the ladders.

Ruben was covering expenses, so there was no need to cut corners. His philosophy was that freedom is priceless. But they couldn't afford to fail.

If they did, they would both be on 23-hour lock-down in an isolation cell with only the bars on the ceiling for their daily air. Visits would only be allowed behind glass and the screws would use all kind of irritating measures to get their revenge. This could go on for a few years, so a mistake would be very costly in these terms!

As the plan was slowly coming together, piece by piece, Londoño was getting extremely anxious about the whole situation. He had a very sharp business mind, but he didn't have the criminal instinct Brendan had. Once the first ladder touched the outside prison wall, the camera and sensors would activate the general alarm. What was unknown was how the screws would react. Would they lock the prison down at the first sound of the alarm, or would they wait to hear why the alarm had been triggered on their radios?

The gym was the best location to break out. Once the alarm went off and in the gym, it would be possible to receive the gun through the window and use the weapon to hold back the screws. Londoño was afraid the screws would jump them first. Usually there were four screws in the gym room, plus two instruction screws. They were so arrogant, but Brendan reassured him that when it was happening, they would back off. It would take one to one and a half minutes for all the ladders to be in place and the gun passed in. Also the screws in the gym would be too confused for a minute or so. That would be enough time to get away.

The bent screw who did the letter dropping was beginning to ask for more jobs. He said he would do anything for money, but he had served his purpose for now and wasn't needed for anything now except the letters. It's always worth keeping these people sweet so Brendan told him when something was going on, he'd let him know.

Eventually Brendan convinced Londoño that the escape had to be from the cantilever windows of the gym. These windows were nearly always locked. But very occasionally, when the air was really stale and stuffy, prisoners would ask for permission to open the window a bit. An instructor screw would pass the question on to a unit screw, who would make clear by a simple gesture of the head whether he allowed it or not. Mostly he nodded yes. An open cantilever window meant however nothing more than a chink of a few inches on top of the window. Two latches on either side prevented them from opening more. But with a small technical action, it was possible to open the window completely, but this was strictly prohibited.

A few days before Christmas a date was pencilled in for the second week in January. The outside help was ready for it. They had a precise map of where to come in and place the aluminium ladders. First, they would place a ladder against the outside wall to climb it and to put the second ladder on the inside wall. The third ladder would be placed under the window of the gym. Every letter contained coded instructions. Certain words used on the phone confirmed each piece of the plan was in place.

Writing an encoded letter was a piece of cake and something Brendan had perfected over many years. For example, he could talk for hours with his brother Tony about the planning of an escape without anyone noticing it. People who heard the conversation would just think they are talking about shopping or football. There were many ways to exchange information secretly. When writing an encoded letter, he would put the time on top. For example, February 19, 11.30 a.m. This number 11 was the key; the reader knew that he only had to remember every 11th word of the letter. The 22nd word was the second word, the 33rd word the third, and so on. If you put all these words in a row, it made a sentence, like: Next-Monday-at-half-past-one-I-need-a-car-a-driver-and-two-handguns. But to the unitiated, this letter seemed to contain innocent, chatty information. It's as simple as can be: from the best secured prisons it's possible to just send letters with every single detail of an escape, without anyone ever intercepting the information. And in every jail, it's possible to buy yourself a personal screw who delivers this letter for you or accomplishes other missions you have in mind.

On the EBI wing the routine was as strict as day one, except for one thing: it was extremely stuffy and sweaty on the unit. Everyone complained about it. The screws didn't have an explanation for it. 'We're also sweltering' they said. A wave of panic came over Brendan as he realised what was causing the stuffiness. The air vent in the shower! When he had squashed it, it had broke. Hopefully they would be out before it was straightened out.

Fortunately, there had been no incidents or security scares to alter the routine at night in the cells. Each night Brendan lay on his bed in the dark and went over everything in his mind. The whole escape depended on a calm routine during the escape. The helpers outside the prison who were arranging the escape were perfectionists.

As the moment of truth approached, the bent screw was rewarded with a bonus he could pick up at a certain address. It always involved cash money. The banknotes were wiped and cleaned carefully, so that no single fingerprint was left on it. The screw seemed happy enough. He didn't have the foggiest notion of what we were up to and how important his role he was.

Besides the two potential escapees there was only one person in De Geerhorst who was acquainted with every detail of the escape plans; the Catholic priest. The only thing he didn't know was the date of the break out. The priest never broke his professional secrecy!

Everything seemed to be in place and ready to go until one day Brendan made what could've been a costly error by clashing with a screw in the unit. He had bit his lip already a couple of times with him but on this occasion he was unable. The officer had a handlebar moustache, which he entered into competitions with, and would gel it. In Brendan's book, if it walked like a duck and quacked like a duck, then it's probably a duck and this screw was real prick. He would go out of his way to annoy people. Normally Brendan could put up with it. The screws were just doing a job; they were just prisoners doing time. Nothing personal, you should say, but that's not how it is in jail. Of all the people who work in these places, 98% don't understand anything about dignity and self-respect.

This particular morning, Brendan was going into the workshop to put plastic clips together, when the moustache-screw started shouting 'You're ten minutes late'. Glancing at him he sarcastically replied: 'Yes, I missed the bus.' The screw didn't see the funny side and carried on shouting. For Brendan it was the last straw, after so many annoying experiences with this guy he put his hand up and said: 'Stand in the corner and not another word, or I'll cut your moustache off'. The screw did what he was told, knowing he would lose his moustache if he didn't. After an hour of work it was time to go and the screw was warned: 'If you rat on me, I will take it very personally'. Whatever he said or did, the incident was never mentioned again.

In one way he was glad he'd shut this screw up, but Brendan was also annoyed with himself for jeopardising the escape. He could easily have been put in isolation for a long time.

Christmas came and went. January 1992 was wet and cold, the 14th was the date set for the escape. Everything was ready. Four cars would be used to get from Sittard to Amsterdam. There were two safe houses in Amsterdam and one halfway, in case they needed to get off the road. The weapons in the car were two Uzi machineguns, one high power Browning and the other Browning would be the one passed on in the gym for the escape. The first three 9mm bullets were blanks to scare off any 'hero' screws. The next nine were 'lives'. Nobody was stopping them going out.

Once over the main outside wall, associates could put a ladder on the factory workshop roof by the main gate and use the roofs of the joined factories to run along. The roofs were joined as far as the EBI; a security blunder that allowed the ladder to be slid under the rolls of razor wire, allowing a person to climb under the ladder and pass in a gun. The gym was ideal for it. At least, if it all worked out the way they'd planned it…

# Chapter Three: Moment of Truth

They woke up that morning with their minds fully focused on the evening and the escape. Following the daily routine both men tried to appear normal. Brendan was looking forward to getting out of the jail and the country. The phone call that day confirmed everything was going ahead as planned.

One of the main concerns was the police. It wasn't known if the alarm was connected through to the police and what procedure would be followed, what roads would be blocked and how fast they would react. It would be entirely up to them to get out of the way though because neither man was going with them while there was firepower. How the screws reacted didn't really matter.

Ruben was quite tense all day and Brendan had to say on more than one occasion 'Don't worry. Things will be okay if we stick to plan'.

Tea time lock up came. This was the last opportunity to relax and prepare mentally for the evening's event. Laying down in the dark Brendan tried to clear his mind to just concentrate on the escape. Deep down he was hoping nobody would be hurt, but if it was necessary, then so be it. At only 28 years old he just couldn't accept spending years living in a cell.

The cell door was opened for evening gym and as Brendan stepped outside, he took in all the details. Things appeared normal on the unit. Screws were their usual arrogant selves, full of confidence with their illusions of superiority. He allowed himself a smile at what was in store for them! On the way to the gym Brendan passed the other two, Joe & Husnu and was able to quietly say: 'Wouldn't it be nice to leave this place and just be out?'

Nothing more was mentioned, but he knew when things start happening, they would know they were invited. So, if they wanted to follow, they could. It was all right with them.

All the usual security was in place. The sets of screws were sitting at various points. As the men began warming up four screws stood watching them near the door. The two sports screws walked round and helped Husnu and Joe on the bench. Brendan had just taken the weights off a barbell, left the fifteen kilo bar on the floor and set up a little circuit when right on time Ruben asked to open the top of the window. The senior screw nodded a yes. So far, so good. A 'no' would have meant smashing the window to get to the Browning 9mm.

As the seconds ticked to the time of the escape, 7.45 p.m everything was ready. Then suddenly a siren started going off and spotlights came on. The screws all started looking at their bleepers and the radios were buzzing. The sound of hard shoes running towards the gym could be heard in the distance. The screws looked confused and worried. They were all talking and shouting at once. A minute had passed. In the next ninety seconds, the ladder should be slid down in front of the window. Thirty slow seconds ticked by. The alarm seemed louder by the second. The gym door opened and the screws exchanged rapid words. Ruben had by now managed to open the window completely. Joe and Husnu watched what was happening, petrified with fear. In the cacophony of voices, the senior screw shouted: 'Lock down high-risk prisoners!'

Bending down, Brendan picked up the barbell. As the screws were all coming towards us, he swung it and shouted: 'Come on bastards!! Come on!!' They backed off. The two instruction screws backed off too, both heading towards the door at the same time. As he raised the iron bar the screws were putting their hands up from a distance, saying: 'Please, Brendan. Don't do anything stupid'.

Ruben stood near the window. The helpers were on time. Holding the bar in his right hand, Brendan reached in and took the FN Browning with his left through the window. As they saw the weapon, the screws pulled back to the hall as fast as they could. Just like Joe and Husnu. They stayed behind in De Geerhorst, not knowing how the screws were going to react. The escapees had thought it would be a case of having to hurt some of them, but no, they were gone out the door in seconds, running up the corridor.

Out of the window, Ruben first, and then up the first ladder. They were on the roof. All the spotlights and alarms were on. Running across the other side of the roof they looked for the other ladder. 'There it is!', Ruben pointed with his finger. He went down first. Brendan immediately followed him, but the ladder was too weak to carry two people and broke. Both men fell heavy. Ruben sprained his ankle and it ballooned up. He couldn't stand on it. Brendan landed on his back and was winded for a few seconds. Ruben had to be dragged and carried to the next ladder. Expecting dozens of screws to be running around any second, there were none. They must have thought the men were heavily armed with guns and stayed away.

The ladder against the inside wall looked sturdy enough, but after the earlier falls neither man wanted to take any risk. 'Easy, Ruben. You first', offered Brendan. He got up the ladder, despite the pain is his ankle. When he reached the top, it was Brendan's turn. On top of the wall they were able to take a good look around. Not a soul. As the adrenalin pumped through his veins Brendan hoped they hadn't been set up by someone in the communication or whatever, a bug, fuck knows. He could smell freedom.

Once they were down the last ladder on the outside wall they knew they had to turn right from facing forward, then run to the end of the grass, onto the gravel. When their feet touched the gravel, they had to go left and run to a hedge and crawl through a prepared hole in it. Behind this hedge would be the first high-powered car waiting.

Because Ruben's ankle was sprained, Brendan had to support and run with him. It was going alright as they ran along the grass, but when they hit the gravel both men fell because they were running too fast. Getting up they ran along the gravel towards the hedge. It must've looked pretty comical and both men were laughing as they ran. Eventually they got through the hedge, into the car and sped out of the area onto the main road to Amsterdam.

Both men lay in the back. Ruben was buzzing and laughing, but Brendan wasn't happy yet. They still had a fair distance to go to Amsterdam and there could be roadblocks. The other two people in the front of the car were experienced. They knew what they were doing and knew the dangers. Ruben was just happy to be out.

**'From the penitentiary for long-serving prisoners in Sittard, De Geerhorst, two heavy criminals escaped last night. The fugitives are a 28 years old Irishman and a 40 years old Colombian. Both are considered armed and dangerous. Around 8.00 p.m. the two men got assistance from the outside, when five armed men climbed over the wall using a ladder. Three of them were arrested, but the two others managed to escape. The police raied the alarm and searched the area without any positive result.'**
*Source: De Telegraaf, Wednesday 15th January, 1992.*

The passenger was explaining how they recruited the helpers. They had pulled into Amsterdam Central Station and asked some guys if they wanted to make some money, 20,000 guilders each. They showed the money, said it wasn't hard and took four men in the van with them. They paid each of them their money, 80,000 guilders in all, and drove to Sittard in silence. During the ride the four men tried one by one to make conversation with them and to find out what kind of job they had been paid to do, but their employers had kept tight lipped. Brendan and Ruben couldn't help laughing about this story, imagining how the four guys must have felt, wondering what was happening.

Apparently when they pulled up to the jail, two of the men were so frightened they wanted to give their share of 20,000 guilders back, but it was made clear that this was not the deal. They had to place the first and second ladder against the outside and inside wall. The third ladder they had to run with to the building and hand in the gun. Then they had done their job and could leave. There were two hired cars left in the car park for them to go in.

**'It's not clear how long the helpers were busy putting the ladders in place, because no one witnessed them. Immediately after the escape the prison's sports instructor activated the alarm. The police arrived quickly enough to arrest three men who are suspected of assisting. They are Antilleans who remained silent during the interrogation by the police.'**
*Source: Algemeen Dagblad, Thursday 16th January, 1992*

Before reaching Amsterdam they changed cars, arriving in the city pretty quickly. The two escapees were dropped off in a street and made their way to a safe house, where they were greeted by a woman and man, who lived in the house. They were nice people and made them welcome. Rubens put his very swollen ankle in a bowl of cold water. In the few months they had spent together Ruben

had never looked so relaxed. He looked at Brendan and said: 'Amigo, from my heart and from my family, I thank you for this escape'.
'Ruben, I was going out anyway. It's nice to help someone in the same bleak situation as we were in. So it's alright.' Replied Brendan.
'No', he said, 'It was much more than that. I want you to come to Colombia with me. I promise you won't regret it!'
'Maybe I will come over for a few months to let things in Europe die down, but first I have a couple of things to do'.
'Like what? Is it worth risking being in jail again?' Ruben asked. Brendan shrugged. 'Nothing is worth being in jail, but sometimes things must be done'.
'You know why I was in jail?' Ruben asked.
'Coke'
'Yes. Thousands of kilos. Lots of money. But I was in jail because of one greedy man. He had asked for £25,000 for 'protection', but he had already been paid. This guy claimed he needed more money for expenses to make sure they were left alone. It was pure blackmail. I refused to pay the money. In fact, this £25,000 was nothing to me, but I just didn't want to be fooled around with. My reaction was emotional. Really, I could pay the extra money easily. I wish I had done that'.

After a couple of days in the house the two men parted and Brendan assured Ruben he would phone him on the number he gave, to make sure he got home alright.

**'Directly after the escape, according to the Amsterdam Solicitor General Mr. R.J. Manschot, the authorities at the airports in surrounding countries were asked to look out for the Colombian, who still holds the European record on smuggling cocaine. Also the intelligence-liaison-members in South-America try to find a trace of the man, but so far in vain.'**
*Source: NRC Handelsblad, Saturday 2nd January 1993.*

Ruben fled into Spain via Belgium and France. Then he was like a fish in water. Brendan, however had to make a plan to liberate his brother from jail. Tony was still behind bars due to the armed robberies and the tram hijacking in Amsterdam. Ruben had left £20,000 for Brendan and he used this money to buy everything needed for the attempt to release Tony: a big Yamaha motorbike, a couple of ladders and passports. A safe house was also procured near the jail.
'Brendan, say the amount you need and I will give it to you', Ruben had said. Brendan accepted the £20,000 but wouldn't take more as he had plenty of ideas where he could get his own money. He preferred to do things himself and not on someone's back. After a robbery or two he knew he would have enough money to live for a while. He just had to find out where to do these robberies.

# Chapter Four: The C1000 Supermarket

Over the following couple of months Brendan looked around for a decent robbery. A million guilders would be nice. He eventually settled on two targets: a supermarket and a bank. Early in the morning he would rob the supermarket, the C1000 in North-Amsterdam. After that he would head to the Rabobank in centre of Amsterdam. Yes indeed, the Rabobank, pronounced as rob a bank...

In the safe of the C1000 there would be 500,000 guilders after Easter weekend. The person who had told him about it was an employee of the supermarket, a relative of a friend of his. In the bank there would even be one million guilders waiting for them. It would be enough to lead a carefree life somewhere else. Brendan had decided he wanted to leave Holland after this job. But first he had to release Tony. He would have done the same for him.

To look Dutch, Brendan had dyed his hair blonde. He bought two cars: a BMW 525i which he got tuned up, and an Opel. He rented a flat a few feet from a big cop shop in West Amsterdam and moved in. Sometimes it was best to be near the police. They only seemed to start looking far from the station and not on their doorstep. He knew they thought he was out of Holland. A friend who knew a bent cop working in Amsterdam had got the latest news and according to this information they were working on the assumption he had been gone from Holland a few days after the escape.

Brendan had been out looking at the jail and was happy with it. The escape would be easy: just one wall and a fence between him and the exercise yard. Against the outside wall and the fence, a ladder could be put with a role of rope ladder on top for the inside wall and fence. Tony could run over, climb up the rope ladders, come down the aluminium ladders and then run into the van. In the back of the vehicle were two pieces of wood up against each side of the van to hold the motorbike in place. Also installed was a piece of wood with a lip on it. It could be thrown down, so we could just drive out of the van. The day after the escape we would do the first robbery.

But to the surprise of Brendan, Tony suddenly changed his mind. A visitor of his passed on the message that he wanted to leave it. He thought he shouldn't escape with only a couple of years left. It made sense and Brendan didn't say anything one way or the other, but his decision played on his mind for a few days. He knew him like the back of his hand. It was just important that he would have whatever he needed while he was in there. Brendan had to accept he was on his own again. He didn't mind. It had been more or less that way since his escape from the London jail.

So the escape plan was scrapped and instead Brendan found a beautiful spot near the sea to lay low. It was quiet and discrete; a perfect place to stay a few months. The nervous life he led would never stop as long as he was on the run.

It was a bizarre way of living and at that moment he would have loved to be just normal. It seemed mad to him, especially silly things like going armed with two pieces just to buy bread and milk or a burger. It was on his mind to settle down, have a normal job, a normal home and a normal family. But his life just wasn't like that. He wondered what it was like being just able to sleep carefree, without worrying if the door would be smashed in. There was always that doubt that they knew where he was, it didn't matter what country he was in. He realised there would always be a poxy fucking cell in some unit reserved for him.

Brendan met and spoke with the employee that was giving information on C1000. From what he said it seemed to be OK in respect to the security and he answered all of the questions put to him. All that remained was to check it out in person.

Brendan already had two British guys in mind, Colin and Chap. They were ready for action so the three men dropped in to see a contact in North Amsterdam. He didn't ask any questions and didn't mind them using the flat as a kind of base. He knew he would be paid for his hospitality.

The newly formed team then followed the manager of C1000 to his house in Ilpendam to see if they possibly could capture him over there. The men would take him to the supermarket and force him to open the safe. It was, however, a bad spot. Too out in the open. Anyone might see him being taken. Also, the manager seemed cagey and nervous so it was decided to take him down at the C1000. This was the man who knew all the alarm codes and had the combination and keys to the safe. He was crucial to the plan and it was important to get this bit right.

They mapped out the area of the supermarket. The roads were good roads for speed. A couple of dry runs were made and two different routes were planned, A and B. Obviously it was hoped that they wouldn't need route B but if the police showed up it was the one they would have to take.

It was still dark when Brendan, Colin and Chap got into the car for the final dry run. In the early hours North Amsterdam seemed deserted. Keeping just under the speed limit they drove from the police station Wadden-weg to the C1000 on the Buikslotermeerplein. They'd timed it: sixty seconds. That meant if something went wrong, the police would be outside in less than one minute.

All three men were focused and confident that they could do this job, but it sure was risky. The police station was the biggest in North Amsterdam. There were over one hundred cops stationed there. They had to succeed. On top of that Brendan had been on the run for three months since the escape from Sittard. He couldn't afford to fail and go back to prison.

There were more twenty employees plus office staff present in the supermarket each and every day. They would have to wait until 8.30 a.m. for the time lock on the safe to activate. A security guard had the second key, there would be a lot of people to deal with.

Observing the situation from a distance, at 5.00 a.m. a car turned into the street. It was the manager. He used a side door to enter the supermarket. This was the spot he would be jumped and captured.

The information they'd got from the employee in C1000 was very detailed. On a holiday weekend they took 500,000 guilders or more. On regular days the trade was to be picked up by money transporters, but not on Easter Monday. It would be a perfect moment for a robbery.

It all looked good, except there was a guy who walked his dog every time in the dead of the night. He was very nosey. Twice during the dry runs he'd turned up so it was decided if he turned up on the day of the robbery him and his dog would be brought in too.

Each man would each have his own parts to play. Colin was to watch the people on the floor at all times and keep them quiet. Chap was to wait for the doorbell and let people in. Brendan would be watching all this and making sure the people were not treated any worse than they had to be.The safe house was four miles away. The only way to leave North Amsterdam was through the IJ-tunnel. The plan was to stay a day or two after the robbery and then leave separately.

On Tuesday 21st April 1992 they were ready. The three men would use two seperate cars. The plan was logical but delicate. First, they would overpower the manager. Then as each staff member arrived, they would be let in and then forced to lie them down and keep quiet till the robbers left with the money.

At 4.30 a.m. the three went to the top of the Bovenoven tower block, opposite the C1000. From 30 feet up they had an excellent view on the back of the supermarket. The only cars on the road were taxis and police. Each man carried a handgun and extra bullets. In the second car were two more 9mm semi automatics handguns.

The manager arrived just before 5.00 a.m. He was a little earlier than he had been when observed during the dry runs. It was decided to let him go in. Then he could deal with the security alarm and make the phone call with his security code to indicate that there was nothing out of the ordinary and not to arouse any suspicions. The three robbers then took the lift down. It was time.

As they reached the door another employee arrived. He was a few paces ahead and as he approached the door Brendan pulled down his mask and took out the gun. Colin and Chap did the same. He was told to ring the bell and put his face at the spy hole. Brendan gave him the few seconds for his mind to take in what was happening and then barked: 'Do it now!'

The man obeyed in silence and a few seconds later the door was opened. Before the manager knew what was happening the employee had been pushed inside and three masked me were pointing guns at him.

'Good morning. We're here for the money. If you co-operate with us, you'll not be hurt' said Brendan calmly but firmly.

After it had sunk in, it was explained to the manager what was to happen. He was told in no uncertain terms that if he tried to fuck around he would be shot. Then they went over the alarm codes with him, which surprised him a bit when he realised that the robbers already knew his codes. He was asked about the safes, but he only told them what they knew already, except for one detail: he said he thought there would be 300,000 guilders, not 500,000 guilders. If this was true it would be very disappointing to all three men who had so much riding on this.

The doorbell was ringing. Two people were outside. Chap stood at the front door watching as Brendan let them in, closed the door behind them and pointed his gun to where Colin was waiting. 'Lie down, keep quiet and mind your own business!' they were told.

After repeating this several more times, the increasing number of people was beginning to be a problem. They were being laid down in the store room, but there wasn't much room left. There was still two hours to wait until 8.30 a.m. Only then the safe would be unlocked automatically.

There must have been going on about sixteen people, when Brendan took the manager down to look at the safes. Chap stayed at the door. Having watched Brendan do this job many times already, he said he would be fine. Colin was alright too. Everyone was lying down quietly, their faces turned to the wall. Colin was walking up and down watching them. He would also watch and make sure that Chap didn't have problems at the door.

There was a bit of concern around Chap and Brendan, in particular, didn't have the best of faith in him. He was fond of drinking and Brendan had made it clear in the early planning stages that he didn't want any drinking for at least three days before the job. Chap hadn't really liked that, but who cared what he liked. That's the way it was. They couldn't afford any mistakes.

Colin spoke a little Dutch and spoke to the hostages: 'Is everyone ok? Don't worry, you won't be harmed. Once they do what we ask we'll leave with the money'. They all answered that they were alright. A couple were sobbing, some shaking, but they were doing okay.

The manager was told to lead the way to the front cash office with Brendan. The shop itself was very big. At the front were several offices over-looking the car-park, on the busy main road. Like many big supermarkets there were windows instead of walls on each side. From the outside people could easily see what was happening inside. For that reason Brendan concealed the gun down by his side and removed his mask. Once in the cash room and away from prying eyes normal service would be resumed, but in the meantime the manager was ordered to keep his eyes closed.

In the cash office was a big safe, with both a combination and a key lock. 'Open it' the manager was told and a few seconds later Brendan got his first look inside the safe. On one shelf was a cash bag. Also inside was another strong box, this compartment contained the main money. He was reminded of the EBI jail: a prison within a prison. The security guard, who would arrive at

8.30 a.m, would have the key to the strong box. Only he could open it. To make everything look as normal as possible to passers by, some of the employees were put onto the tills and given shelf stacking duties. If things were too quiet the security guard would know something was wrong.

Meanwhile there were six big delivery lorries parked outside with others waiting, ready to get unloaded. 'These guys want to come in. What do we do now?', Chap asked. The drivers were beginning to lose their patience. They also blocked the escape route. Something had to be done.

'We'll take the drivers in and get their keys', Brendan said, thinking on his feet. 'Chap and I will go out at 8.00 a.m. to drive the lorries into the big car park. Colin can control the place until we're back. Then we we'll wait for the security guard'.

Before leaving to deal with the lorries Brendan asked the manager why he thought there was only 300,000 guilders. 'That is the average taking on bank holidays', he answered. It seemed likely that the 'super-informer' had just been trying to boost up the figures so it would be more of an interest to us. There would be serious repercussions if this was the case but in less than two hours they would know for certain how much money was there.

## Chapter Five: Taking Hostages

Suddenly there was the sound of someone running towards the cash office. It was Chap, seized by panic. 'The bell just rang', he gasped, 'but when I opened the door, there was no one there!'
'Have you looked outside?' Brendan asked.
'No' Chap answered. 'I just ran straight to you'.
How fucking stupid was that? Brendan couldn't believe it.
'Go to the safe and bring back the manager!' he called, while running to the door. By the time he arrived nobody was outside, but something wasn't right. It was too quiet. Silent, there was no traffic in the street. Brendan went back inside and shouted to Colin: 'Check the front from the upstairs office!'
A minute later Colin came running down. His message was no surprise.
'Cops! Everywhere! The car park is crawling with cops!'
The police had been alerted by the C1000-employee who sometime earlier had rung the bell and then disappeared. Due to Chap's slow reaction, the employee had apparently sensed danger. Somehow he managed to get a glimpse inside. He could see Chap, masked and armed, and his colleagues lying on the floor. The guy then ran straight to the street, stopped a city bus and made the driver alert the police.
'Watch everyone. I'm going upstairs to take a look', Brendan shouted at Colin and Chap.
There were about seven offices that overlooked the car park. Brendan ran into the second office. It had two big windows with blinds pulled up. Going to the corner of the window he looked out. There were police all over the place, their guns drawn and crouched behind cars. Others were running to their positions. More policemen were arriving by the minute. They were in big trouble if they didn't move now. Taking another good look he could see there were at least thirty to forty cops between the C1000 and the two getaway cars.
In advance they'd talked about this scenario. If things went wrong, they would take hostages and get to the cars and drive route B, which consisted partly of a narrow long road on the route. One of the men would get into the second car follow the first one and, once on the narrow street, just handbrake it and turn the wheel. The car would slam into the parked cars on each side, blocking the road. Then the driver would jump into the front car. This car had already been tuned up. It was a racing monster. Before the police got the car out of the way, they would be out of the second car.
Running back downstairs Brendan told Colin and Chap what they needed to do. He could tell by their eyes that they weren't very enthusiastic. Chap even less so. Trying to take hold of the situation Brendan told him he had a choice: either do it his way, or they'd end up in jail for a long time. End of discussion. Each minute they wasted talking gave the cops more time to strengthen their position. Colin agreed, but Chap was not OK. Taking Chap aside Brendan told him: 'Listen. Look at it this way: the worst thing that can

happen is that you're shot dead'. Chap didn't seem to get the humour.
'Are you coming or staying?' barked Brendan but Chap wanted to know again how it was going to work with the hostages.
'We'll take one hostage each to the cars. Two of us get in with their hostage. One of us will wait with his hostage until both cars are started. Once this has happened, they'll get in as well. Then, and only then, will we release the other hostages with the instruction to run in different directions.'
'What about the police?' Chap asked.
'Just ignore them, do what you have to do'.

Chap just wasn't up to it. He was on about breaking through to the basement next door. There was no next door. Finally Brendan snapped.
'Colin, you and I will go' he said. Colin nodded. For the first time there was now tension between the gang. Chap was really pissing the others off. They needed to make their case to the police and explain how it was going to work. Brendan grabbed the manager: 'Come with me. If you don't do what you're told, I will blow your brains out!'

Wrapping his hand around the manager's tie with the gun to his head. Brendan opened the door and stepped outside with him. There were police every which way they looked. Just at the front was a cop who looked like he was in charge. He had at least ten men around him, guns drawn and pointed towards the two men who had just emerged from the supermarket. Shuffling in his direction Brendan asked:
'Are you in charge here?'
'Yes', the cop answered.
'What's your name?'
'Gerard. And yours?'
'Ok, Gerard. This is the way it's happening. I will not negotiate on it. First tell all of your cops to put their guns down, or I will shoot the manager'. The cop stared for a few seconds and said something in Dutch. They all put there guns back in their holsters. This was positive.
'We've got sixteen hostages!' Brendan shouted to the head cop. 'We're about to leave. It'll be your responsibility if anyone gets shot.'
'No way it's my responsibility', he answered.
'Listen, all we want to do is leave. So, if you try to stop us, we'll start shooting everyone around us.'
It was pure bluff, but bluffing was the only chance to get out of this terrible situation.

Brendan moved backwards through the door, still holding the manager to his body. Once inside the manager was told to face the wall while Brendan explained to the other two that they would move now, but only Colin was there.
'Where's Chap?'
'He's looking for a way out onto the roof' Colin answered.
Here they were, in a detached building, on its ground floor. No matter what side

of the roof they jumped off, they were surrounded by police. And this fellow Chap was on the top floor looking for a way onto the roof, whilst the only real chance they had was slipping away by car. If they didn't do what they'd said to the police now, their position would be much weaker. A special police squad could be here any moment now.

It was 7.30 a.m. Eventually they found Chap at the roof skylight peeping out. 'What the fuck are you doing? We've got to go now!' shouted Brendan, but he said he was too nervous to go out like that. Walking back down the stairs, it was now Colin's turn to throw a spanner in the works.

'I won't go without Chap', he said. All three were almost certainly going to jail now if they couldn't bluff their way out!

This was quickly turning into one bad situation. Even all the hostages were talking. Some of them were escorted to the back to use the toilet. They may as well be comfortable and they were allowed to sit upright. Several of them asked for cigarettes, drinks and a bite to eat. Brendan said he would sort it out soon.

The phone rang. It was the police. Brendan agreed to come out and speak to the head cop and he told Colin to walk behind holding a hostage with him.

'Tell the police in Dutch that if I'm shot, they will start shooting the hostages inside.' shouted Brendan at Colin. No one seemed to understand Colin's shouting in a deafening mix of Scottish and broken Dutch. As they walked towards the police chief they were unaware that the Dutch media had arrived on the scene and were broadcasting everything live on national television.

As they approached the chief cop undid the strap on his holster. So, Brendan tucked his jacket in behind his back, exposing his gun. The cop said something like give up this hopeless situation, release the hostages and so on. Brendan took out a packet of cigarettes, as cooly as he could manage, given the situation they were in.

'Smoke?' he asked.

'I don't smoke', the man said.

'Listen, Gerard. We want a helicopter to land on the roof with enough room for us and three hostages. But not until we say so.  First, we will wait for the time lock on the safe to open for the money. And we also want money off of you's.'

'I'll have to discuss this with my boss', he reacted.

'Next time bring someone in with authority, Gerard.'

He could tell the robbers had the upper hand. Brendan told him that if he arranged their demands, as a show of good faith, they'd would let one hostage go.

When the men went back in, they explained to the others what had been said. Colin brought the ones who wanted to go to the toilet one by one, while Brendan went with the manager for food, snacks and drinks.  At the deli counter he couldn't believe his ears when the manager said, pointing to the

cheeses: 'These are very expensive.' Smiling at him Brendan replied: 'To hell with expensive! Fill the tray with it and get some rolls. Do it now!'
A few seconds later there were sixteen people sitting down with food, drinks and cigarettes.

Once the hostages were a bit more comfortable Brendan went to check the front offices. Putting one of the market coats on, he took his hood down and held his hands up as if someone was behind pointing a gun at him. Suddenly, as he reached the fourth office along he saw a cop from the special squad, crawling on his hands and knees. He'd entered the office by taking the bottom window out. Lying on his belly, he pulled his gun and raised it as quick as lightning. From two just a few feet away Brendan was looking down the barrel of his Glock. But because of his appearance the cop thought he was a hostage, lowered his gun and whispered something in Dutch, which Brendan didn't really understand. But he was able read the body language, which said something like: 'Quick, get out!' Brendan motioned behind him as if to say he couldn't. At that moment the two men's eyes met then, and it was that look that gave everything away. While the cop still held his Glock down, Brendan grabbed the Browning out of his belt. Immediately the cop pointed his gun to him. This guy was very fast. As they looked into each others barrels Brendan could see in his eyes he wasn't afraid, despite the overwhelming tension of that moment.

Brendan twisted quickly back behind the door panel and knelt down. Looking back, it was a stupid thing to do as the cop could easily have shot him right through the thin plaster wall. Brendan chanced a look round the door and could see him moving back towards the window. A second later he looked again and he had made it back outside. He shouted something like 'Give it up!'

With this moment of danger passed, for now at least, Brendan went back down. It was obvious now that the police were trying to see what was going on inside the place. After explaining what had happened, Brendan told the others: 'Okay, one hostage can go. Then we will relocate them.'

Lying down on the floor a girl was sobbing. 'Why not let her go?', Colin suggested. Brendan hadn't noticed her before. She turned out to be the daughter of the cookie supplier. Her name was Wendy and she was fourteen years old. On this day of her Easter holiday she had decided to spend it with her father. 'Alright, pick her' Brendan agreed. Colin grabbed her and began to move her but she kept saying something in Dutch. 'She wants the older lady to come along with her', Colin translated. After a short discussion the men agreed and the two were allowed to leave. A moment or two later the girl's father was also released.

**'After the police had cordoned off the area, a police sergeant managed during the negotiations with the kidnappers to get seven people free. B. Welten, Chief of the Central Investigation Service in Amsterdam: 'The hostages who were not able to control themselves sufficiently, were**

**permitted to leave first. Apparently, the robbers intended to prevent a panic situation'.**
*Source: Algemeen Dagblad, Wednesday 22nd April 1992*

The rest of the hostages were then moved, because the girl and woman would tell them exactly everything they had seen. Some people were put along the stairs between the offices upstairs and where the men had now positioned themselves downstairs. So, if the police decided to raid the super-market it would be too dangerous for them to come down through the people. Four younger employees were told to put masks on and they were positioned at various points towards the front of the shop. This way they hoped to discourage the cops from entering the building. It was also meant to confuse them how many robbers were there.

While Colin kept an eye on the hostages, Brendan took the manager back to the safe and opened the big door. Taking the cash bag out he left the unopened main safe. There was no way the cops were going to let the guard walk in with the other key. Opening the bag it was clear there was not a lot in it; mainly banknotes of 25 guilders. Taking the bag back to the other two Brendan told them the bad news that the main money was in the safe strong box. They both looked like they were ready to throw the towel in.

By now, some hostages were standing and talking, others were walk-ing around. Two of the four guys that had been put in masks were moved to stay in other positions. The manager walked over. 'What are you going to do?' he asked. As Brendan looked at him he noticed properly for the first time that he was exactly what a manager would be expected to look like. Average build, glasses, moustache. He had the air of someone who knew everything would be alright, despite the potential danger. 'We're still waiting for the other money' he answered.

Two or three of the younger hostages were helpfully getting drinks and cigarettes. Motioning them over, Brendan gave them a few thousand guilders. 'This is stress money' he told them. They hid it on them gratefully and asked if they could help. Brendan laughed. 'No. Just go over there and keep out of the way'.

Colin was getting visibly restless now and asked what to do. 'Time has passed since I said we should move' replied Brendan. 'The best we can do is hope for a deal'. Deep down both men knew this was becoming increasingly unlikely.

Meanwhile, Chap had gone into a mini depression. Brendan decided to check the offices upstairs again. Half expecting another confrontation he was relieved to find all was quiet. He'd only gone a few minutes when Colin called up. 'Some police officer's calling on the phone'. He ran down and grabbed the receiver. 'Give it up', the message was once again.

Because the situation was now so serious the men decided to seek some legal advice. Brendan had a lawyer, who stood had by him after the escape from the EBI at Sittard. "Phone him and get him connected with me" he shouted. All he could think of was that horrible prison in Sittard. He knew they would send him back to a similar one. It was confusing. He needed time to think. Walking up and down the different aisles in the shop he racked his brains. As he passed a shelf of hotdog tins he took one off the shelves and opened it. After emptying it he stuffed it with a few thousand guilders. Then he did it again with another tin. It was just a gesture really but it made him feel better. If he didn't win, they wouldn't win either. It's funny how the mind reacts on confusing situations like that.

As Brendan walked back down to the others he could see Chap was missing once again. After offering Colin a cigarette he asked what he looked so serious about, as if everthing already happening wasn't enough!
'Chap gave himself up a few minutes ago'. Brendan couldn't believe it and went to the door. As he looked out, sure enough Chap was lying face down with his hands stretched out.
'Where's Chap's gun?' Brendan asked Colin.
'I don't know', Colin said.
'What are your plans now, Brendan?'
'What about yours?'
'Fair play to Chap. I won't let him down'.
'Whatever you want, Colin. At this point the only thing we'll get by staying in here is we'll be shot'.
Colin smiled and the two shook hands. 'I'm sorry for how it's gone, Bren'.
'It's okay' Brendan replied as Colin turned and walked to the door. There were some shouting commands and then nothing. Peering through the spy hole Brendan could see Colin outside lying next to Chap. Turning round he walked over to the phone to call a cousin, but when he saw all the faces of the hostages he realised how bad his position actually was. Shaking his head he smiled and told the manager that everybody just had to stay where they were and that the police would come soon.

As he walked slowly to the door all Brendan could feel was sadness at the prosepct of having to go back to jail. He pushed the door open and walked out. Immediately there were shouts to throw the gun down. He did what they said, there was nothing else he could do, and laid next to Colin and Chap. As he turned his head all he could see everywhere were police, machine guns, rifles, handguns, the whole bunch.

The seconds turned into minutes, and the minutes felt like hours. Still the police hadn't come over to them. It must have been close to twenty minutes before they came. Then it became clear why it had taken so long.
'Where are the others?' they asked. They were talking about the employees who had been made to stand around with masks on and clearly thought there were more robbers still at large. Eventually they came over, pointed guns at the

heads of the three men and cuffed them. After being searched and hooded up they were put us in separate cars. Just a few seconds later they were in that big cop shop Waddenweg that they'd driven from a couple of days before to check out the job.

Brendan was held in police custody for ten days. On the first day the hatch opened and all he could see was a pair of eyes. He immediately knew though that they were the same eyes he'd seen in the C1000, during the confrontation with the cop that had crawled in. 'I could see in your eyes that you weren't going to shoot', he said. 'That's why I didn't either'. Brendan just smiled and thought: How wrong can you be! I would have shot him all over the place!'

To begin with he didn't have a clue how much attention the robbery attracted. The newspapers were full of it and everything had been on television as it was happening. He was transferred to De Grittenborgh prison in Hoogeveen, in the northeastern part of the Netherlands. Back in the EBI unit once again. The thought of it alone was horrible. All those bastards that worked there, letting their frustrations out on the prisoners. It's fucking irritating having to stand there and listen to them.

After the usual reception in the EBI Brendan was handcuffed by the screws. Several doors later they were walking down a corridor where people were in cells on both sides. Suddenly the noise of banging and shouting came from the cells. It sounded like they were watching football and cheering for a goal. It went on a while. One of the screws turned to him and asked what the banging was about. Brendan just shrugged and shook his head. Answering his own question he said 'They're banging and shouting because of you'. Brendan looked at him, thinking this smart fucker was just fooling around with him, but once he was on the unit he realised that the screw was right.

The only other prisoner on the unit was Husnu, who he'd been locked up in De Geerhorst in Sittard. He came over and the two men hugged like they were best friends. 'We've seen the whole hostage thing live on television', he said. 'We knew it was you by the papers and the news. That's why all the prisoners are banging. Everyone is honoured that you're here.' Remarkable. I was just thinking how I would get out of this one…

## Chapter Six: Escape From London

For the moment Brendan found himself back to square one. Here he was, in some cell in the Netherlands. Not that long ago he'd been planning for an anonymous life here, but now millions of people had seen him on television. The fact that he had ended up in this country, was in fact purely accidental.

Back in Ireland he'd done a few years in jail following an armed robbery. At the age of 21 he'd been released from prison but found the Irish police wouldn't leave him alone. On the contrary, they'd clearly decided he had to be punished more. They blatantly followed him and raided the house regularly. In their quest for revenge, they made his life a misery. So he went to London.

Brendan had an Uncle in Wembley, who he hadn't seen for a while so he headed there. He'd always liked him and they got on well. He had a great sense of humour and that night they had a right laugh, going to bed after midnight. Next morning was a sunny day and his wife made a full English breakfast. It was the start of summer.

It was a relief. It hits you as soon as you get to London. The Thames seems to pump itself like adrenalin through the pounding metropolis. In Ireland you won't find a melting pot of nationalities and cultures like London.

Being in London Brendan certainly wasn't going to just waste time. A friend in Ireland had asked him to visit a certain address in the city. The occupant owed the parents of this friend an amount of money for land that had been sold. He was always full of promises, but never paid. If Brendan managed to get the full figure back, he could keep half the amount. That was the agreement.

The debtor was full of apologies when Brendan went to his door. It took him one day to get the money and the money was sent straight back to Ireland. With his half Brendan bought one of those 750cc Yamaha motorbikes. It was ideal for the traffic and for the police. He never stopped for any of them!

After three weeks in London he'd decided to go home. It's funny how things happen though. The day before he was going home he met a girl. She was different from any girl he'd known before and she was beautiful. So, he decided to stay a few more days in London. She was really forward, but seemed shy at the same time. She was fun, always fun and she showed him the city.

Once back in Dublin Brendan went to see the fellow he'd collected the money for. Naturally he was happy to see him and had another proposition. Again, it was a collection job in England, but this time it would be double the money. He still had the £35,000 from before, so to collect another legit debt for £70,0000 was a no brainer.

Brendan asked his friend Jack – his nickname - to go with him in exchange for half. Jack agreed. So, a few days later, they were back in London. The fellow who owed the money said he needed a few days to get the cash ready. While Jack visited his aunt in Richmond, Brendan already knew how he would spend the time. He went to the girl's house and they spent the time together. He was as happy as can be.

Eventually the two men met up together to finish the collection job. Early one morning they rang the bell but the debtor wasn't home. They decided to try again after breakfast, but this attempt had no result either. As they walked away, suddenly police cars turned up from every corner. Before they realised what was happening they were bent over a bonnet and handcuffed. How the police got their information is not known to this day, but both men were arrested over an armed robbery in London. For once Brendan had nothing to do with it.

**'The robbers had thought nothing had been overlooked. They selected a South American businessman with an expensive jewellery collection, wore theatrical tanning cream and droopy moustaches to disguise their pale Irish complexions and waited to strike. They tricked their way into the executive's house in Finchley, north London, while he was out, and tied up his wife and daughter in the bathroom. A woman neighbour arrived and was also bound and gagged. David Lynch, Brendan Quinn and Paul Horan then ransacked the house, grabbed £80,000 of jewellery and fled. Flying Squad officers had been trailing them, however, and a high-speed chase developed along the North Circular Road. Their dash for freedom ended when they ran from the Saab Turbo, threw their guns and the jewellery over a wall and leapt in pursuit. They landed on a patrol car in the compound of Finchley police station, quickly realising their mistake when uniformed officers emerged to investigate. The gang climbed back over the wall, only to be arrested in nearby Victoria Park, where Lynch was found cowering behind a bush.'**
*Source: The Times, Tuesday 27th June 1995.*

Jack and Brendan found themselves in Brixton prison on remand. It was a real dump. There was only one kind of racism in there and that was against the Irish. They were then shipped to a prison called Pentonville in North London and put on an E list, which meant that they couldn't associate with any of the other prisoners on exercise or any other time. All exercise was done alone in the yard and they had to collect their meals after all the others had collected theirs.

At night time they were only permitted to wear shorts in the cell. The clothes from the day - the ridiculous yellow striped jumpsuit, jacket and shoes - had to be put on a chair outside the cells. Everywhere they went after leaving the cell, a screw followed with a book.

On Sunday morning 12th June 1988 Brendan's cell door was opened. 'You want to escape?' someone said. It was a relief when it was not a screw who opened the door but a friendly face. Jack was already outside waiting. In his hands he had the keys to all the cell doors, the six gates between the cell block and the yard. This offer did not need much thought. If he stayed in his cell he would probably be sentenced for something he hadn't done.

Jack had arranged clothes for the five men who were going to attempt the escape. The men put them on and opened the first gates. As they went through these gates and locked them behind, Jack handed Brendan some little bits of bent wire. Locking the doors behind him, he put his hand through the bars and placed these pieces of wire in the keyhole. This worked out fine. It prevented any screw coming after them.

They were carrying their iron beds with them. These would be useful at the finishing stage of the attempt. Suddenly Brendan spotted a screw hanging around the first bottom floor. He was surprised when the screw simply gave a nod and disappeared down the hallway. Raising his eyebrows to the fellow who opened my door Brendan was told "Don't worry. He's been taken care of by the other screw we bought the keys from." Brendan didn't care. All that was important was to get out of that jail and out of England, back to Ireland.

When they reached the final gateway that led to the exercise yard, the huge prison wall came into view. It was so high Brendan wondered whether they'd even be able to scale it. There was a big lip at the top of the wall to make it even more difficult for prisoners to climb over.

Walking towards the last gate with their bed tops, they couldn't believe their ears when some of the prisoners locked in their cells started calling out: 'They're escaping!' They were calling out to the screws and ratting on their fellow prisoners! Soon the alarms were ringing out and there was loads of activity. One man panicked and gave himself up straight away. The decision surprised Brendan, but he didn't really care. It was the decision of a fool. He shouldn't have left his cell in the first place if he hadn't got the bottle to follow it through.

The remaining four got through the last gate and Brendan put his arm through and inserted a couple of bits of twisted wire, enough to stop anyone else using the keyhole. Then they began assembling the bed tops underneath the prison wall, putting the top of the beds together to build a ladder. When all the tops were together – around twenty in number - it reached the top of the wall, but just under the lip. The first two tried to get up and over, but couldn't make it over the lip.

There were maybe thirty or forty screws at the other side of the gate, but it was locked and they couldn't get through it. As Brendan looked at their faces he could see how stressed they looked. These cowardly bastards are at their most dangerous at times like this. If he'd had a pound for each time, he saw them take liberties, he would have enough money for a life time.

Now it was Brendan's turn to try to get up the prison wall. Walking over to the makeshift ladder, he managed to scale it and climbed up. Concentrating on the top of the wall he jumped and wiith his fingers he reached the edge, pulling himself up and clambering upon the wall. Once up he took off his top and hung it down to Jack. Brendan could then pull him up on the wall top.

Meanwhile half the screws had ran around the building and were now running towards them. The sound of the stamping of steel toe capped boots became louder and louder.

The other two lads had by now reached the wall top as well. They jumped first and had a nasty fall. Jack and Brendan could hear them scream. From the top of the wall they could see them them lying on the ground, groaning with pain. Just a few minutes earlier the wall had looked huge when they had stood beside it, but now it looked even higher from the top of it. A smooth, soft landing was already out of the question. To discourage any possible escapers to jump off the wall, sharp, raised bricks had been built into the ground.

As Brendan and Jack stood on the wall, trying to concentrate on where best to jump to minimise injury, the screws started throwing their batons at them, along with anything else they could find. 'Let's jump, Jack!'said Brendan and before the words had even left his lips Jack had turned and jumped off.

Jack had landed on his feet very badly. Now there were three groaning men lying on the ground, and it was Brendan's turn. He jumped and managed to restrict the damage by rolling two or three times. This technique of falling that he'd learned in his younger years from Irish karate-monks, came in handy. As Brendan got to his feet he didn't think Jack looked too bad. Unknown to both men still, was that he had broken two heels.

Just a few yards away a car was waiting. Everyone managed to stumble into it and they sped off. The escape had been well planned and Brendan was glad to have been invited on it.

They first went to a flat, where they could make arrangements by phone. That night they were in a safe house in Kilburn, where they stayed for a week before moving to another house, also in Kilburn.

'Four remand prisoners escaped from Pentonville Prison in north London yesterday by using a makeshift ladder tied with blankets to shin over the wall. The Home Office said the four are believed to have had keys to open doors.They are Brendan Quinn and David Lynch, both aged 25, who faced trial on robbery charges, and Christopher Wright, 24, and John Flanagan, 28, who faced trial on drugs charges.
The Home Office said they had used their bedsteads to build the ladder, tying the pieces together with the blankets.
A fellow inmate at Pentonville, London's oldest prison, saw them climb over the wall and make off in a waiting car.
The Home Office is investigating how the fugitives had obtained the keys. The spokeswoman for the Home Office said they were either from Northern Ireland or the Republic of Ireland.
Scotland Yard said that Quinn and Lynch were considered dangerous and should not be approached.'
Source: The Guardian, Monday 13th June 1988

After three weeks had passed since the escape. Jack and Brendan went back to Dublin. Using fake passports they flew from London to France, then across to Dublin. At the airport they were picked up by a friend and driven to a safe house in Dundalk.

Now it was all very different. Both men were wanted. Everything would be harder: travelling, working, even being in the one place too long would be dangerous. Their lives had changed and not for the better.

Sat around the table in a house in Dundalk they talked with a few trusted friends about the situation. Jack was saying he would rather move around Ireland and stay free like that. But Brendan decided during the discussion that in order to stay out of jail he had to go abroad. 'Fuck it! I've never been abroad before, except for England!' he said.

Brendan had never really been interested in going abroad before, but curiosity and circumstances made it time to go and he decided to go to a place called Portugal. Jack didn't want to come along. He was on about the food and stuff like that. The truth is he never really saw any reason to leave Ireland.

A few months later Jack was arrested. He was sitting in a car and had no way out of it. Jack had a sawn-off shotgun with him and he was sentenced to six years imprisonment for an armed robbery.

Using a false name Brendan visited him in prison and told him 'If you want to escape in Dublin, it's not a problem. I know people who always have access to bent screws. Go abroad and take it easy for a few months.'
'But I don't go out', Jack replied. It came out later that his girlfriend had forbidden him to do anything dangerous.

In Portugal Brendan rented an apartment with a small swimming pool. It was a quiet, lovely few months, broken up once a month or so by a friend who would come over with some money. This way the rent could be paid and he used the rest for living on. Freedom is priceless and after a few months in Portugal Brendan felt the need to move on. He had to bring in some cash.

## Chapter Seven: Target Holland

It had been a relaxing few months staying in Portugal, just near a fishing town called Cascais. Now though it was time to move on and Brendan first went back to Ireland for a few days. Apart from money he needed to see some familiar faces for a while. He couldn't stay long though as he was still on the run after the escape from prison in London.

After a short family visit, he headed for the Continent. With him was a holdall with £25,000 in it, which he'd hidden one day in Ireland. Brendan had got into the habit everywhere he went, to put away money and weapons, just in case. Even today there are still several hotel rooms with a gun and several thousand pounds hidden in them.

He stayed a couple of days in France, bought some handguns from a friend in Belgium and moved on to Rotterdam, Holland. There had been a tip about some work in this city, the casino in the Hilton Hotel. The work was put up through a mutual friend who worked inside and he had promised there would be a huge amount of money waiting for to be picked up. This sizeable loot was the only reason for Brendan's visit to Rotterdam.

From Rotterdam Central Station he took a taxi and asked for a nice place to stay. A few minutes later he was outside Hotel Emma, next door to the cop shop. Despite his bed being just a few yards away from the police office, it seemed alright. He booked in, left the bag with the money under the bed and went out to see what kind of city Rotterdam was.

Two streets away was a hotel which seemed nice. It looked perfect for Brendan's brother Tony and their friend, who were in on this piece of work. He went in to book a room for them for two or three nights and then phoned Ireland, telling them where to come, including the name of the hotel and the name the room was booked under. After that he found himself a nice restaurant, had a little look around town and walked back into the hotel to check if everything was still fine.

But as he drew level with the place he'd booked for the two guys Brendan thought it looked different from other hotels. There were girls in front of it with a kind of exaggerated friendly smile. The Turkish hotel owner stood there laughing. In a flash Brendan realised why the owner had reacted so strangely some time earlier, when he'd checked in for two or three nights. It was a whorehouse! It had just looked like a normal hotel earlier! Brendan hurredly left to phone the two fellows in Ireland, but he was too late: they had left half an hour earlier. There was no way of contacting them until they arrived at this whorehouse they were heading for.

Brendan decided to head back to his hotel to get an early night. Before he went to bed he prepared the door so he could hear it if it was opened. He cleaned the two guns he'd brought in from Belgium, a .357 Magnum with a six-inch barrel and a FN Browning High Power 9mm. They were in good condition and he oiled them and put them under the pillow.

Dealing with guns had become second nature to Brendan. It was just part of life. As a boy, when he'd been taking his dog for a walk up the fields one day he met Tommo and Noel, two older boys from the estate. They had a shotgun, an old revolver and a big bag of ammunition. They asked if Brendan wanted to go shooting with them. He'd had only used a firearm once before this, on his uncle's farm. He had a 12-bore shotgun and a pump action shotgun and Brendan had shot a couple of trees with them.

Brendan joined the two lads and they stayed up the fields, shooting anything around. The barrel of the revolver got very hot from all the firing of it. They crossed the railway track and took a walk. Seeing a few cows in the field, they sneaked up on them and shot two cows. Looking at the dead cows that day, Brendan realised how deadly guns were. Tommo and Noel told him if he wanted to go shooting again, he just had to ask for the guns anytime he wanted.

That night he couldn't sleep, thinking about the cows; how easy it was to kill them. Ever since that day a genuine respect for the power of guns stayed with him.

Next morning the farmer had put the cows on a trailer attached to his tractor to remove them. Brendan watched him drive through the estate with the dead animals, convinced in his mind he would take them back to cook them. At least they didn't go to waste, he thought.

Back in Rotterdam, Brendan had a relaxed night. After getting up he made his way to the whorehouse. Opposite was a cafe and he went in and ordered breakfast and waited. Around 11.30 a.m. his brother and friend pulled up by the whorehouse in a taxi. Brendan never did let them go in, instead saving them the embarrassment he had already been through.

So here they were in Holland. The three of them would do the casino job. The casino was always busy, but seemed to have very little security. There were only a couple of doormen with dicky bows and another couple inside the casino. Over the next few days, Brendan rented a few different accommodations: one flat and three hotel rooms. The flat was at the bottom of Nieuwe Binnenweg and it cost 2,000 guilders a month. The hotel rooms were in different ends of the town. They all stayed in the flat while they had a good look at the casino.

After a while they all realised that they didn't actually fancy the work. The right feeling was lacking. The operation had too many weak spots and the route was too risky. They decided to leave it for the time being. The friend had struck up some kind of thing with a waitress in a restaurant and he said he would stay around with her for a week or so. That suited everyone.

Brendan and Tony went to Amsterdam, just the two of them. It was time to get some money and find a target. With some money they could go somewhere abroad and afford anything they needed. Maybe Portugal was alright to stay in again. It was the most relaxing place on earth.

The taxi dropped them at the Dam square. It was extremely busy with lots of people going about their business. Brendan asked somebody where Central Station was, where they had to get a tram to a friend's place. But first they wanted to look around the city and get two or three places to stay, in case they needed somewhere safe.

First, they booked a room in a hotel for the night. Over the next three days they rented an apartment near Central Station, just five minutes' walk away from it. It was a nice apartment in a quiet road. They also booked a hotel room near the docks in Rotterdam. Brendan had often thought to himself: what a waste of money. But fuck it, security comes first and that always costs money. Freedom was their highest priority.

The brothers had a couple of addresses where a friend of a friend could help them out with identity cards and cars, stuff like that. Tony did the talking, Brendan stayed in the background. There was no point in both showing their faces. Tony bought some ID's and arranged for two cars to be picked up, an Opel and a Volvo. That night they stayed in the apartment and talked about the next job. Would it be a city bank, or would it be better to rob a bank in one of the towns around Amsterdam? Both agreed that they needed a couple of days to look around and think things over. They'd lost faith in the casino robbery in Rotterdam now.

Eventually it was decided to rob a money exchange office in the Leidsestraat, a very crowded shopping street in the centre of Amsterdam. It was to happen on April 2nd 1991. It soon became clear that this job was quite risky, so they had to come up with an alternative second target. Tony came up with an idea. 'The fellow I bought the cars and ID's from told me about a hotel with a complete collection of golden coins, Rolex-wristwatches, cash money and some other things.' It sounded alright for a quick look. Some extra cash would come in alright until a decent robbery came up.

Tony and Brendan left their friend in Rotterdam with his new girlfriend. There was no need to have three people around. The more people involved in the preparation, the more attention would be attracted. He would probably be annoyed, but he would also understand that no one wanted to put any of the others in danger if it could be avoided. They all knew each other very well and were all determined to do what had to be done.

Due to some unforeseen reasons they indeed did have to skip the plans to rob the money exchange office. Instead they went on to plan B: the robbery of Hotel Astoria on the Martelaarsgracht. Early next morning Brendan and Tony went to the hotel, which was close to Central Station. The hotel had a doorbell with an intercom. If the door was opened, you could go upstairs to where the reception was.

Brendan wasn't really keen on this type of robbery. He preferred cash, but money was needed to get money. The hotel robbery was just a stepping stone. As they went upstairs, both men were wearing baseball hats and scarves. They didn't know much about the hotel, only what was in the safe.

After ringing the bell on the counter a woman came out. She looked very masculine and had a deep voice to match. 'How can I help you?', she asked. That was the cue for Brendan and Tony to jump over the counter and pull their guns out. They pushed her back into the office and scanned the area for other people. They were alone, except for two big dogs. 'Tell us the number to the safe!' Brendan commanded. The woman bit back and said she didn't know it. Refusing to accept this Brendan told her they had no intention of leaving before the safe was opened. 'When Ruud comes back, he will go mad!' she shouted.

'And where is this Ruud of yours?' Brendan asked.

'Upstairs' she said.

Leaving Tony with the woman Brendan went one floor up to get Ruud or whatever the fuck he called himself, but he wasn't around. Suddenly from downstairs he heard screams. Running back down, as he went to the room with the safe, he could see his brother and this woman rolling on the bed. In the middle of the fight she had her hand on the Magnum .357. Tony had his hand still on the handle, but was in trouble. Brendan quickly grabbed her wrist and twisted it, the same time taking the piece off her. To avoid any further complications they tied her up, put her on the bed and forced her with the gun against her head to tell the combination of the safe. 'Say it, bitch!', Brendan shouted. She talked.

In the safe was indeed a collection of gold coins. There were about 14.000 guilders in cash and other stuff like Rolexes and so on. It wasn't worth much, but it would do to finance a bigger robbery. As they left they warned the woman 'If you go to the police, we'll come back and kill you!'

Exiting the hotel they walked across to the Nieuwendijk and then into a side street, where they got a tram. They sat separately and just let it go a few stops. After a while though they decided they should get off the tram and stood up to head for the exit. They could hardly believe it when the tram went round a corner and stopped at a tram stop right outside the hotel they had just robbed. There were already half a dozen police there. Brendan looked over at his brother and rolled his eyes as to say 'fuck this'.

They retook their seats again as fast as they could, doing their very best not to attract attention. The tram pulled off again. After waiting for a few stops, they eventually got off and got a taxi to a safe house. While Tony got rid of the collection and other bits, Brendan waited at a café. This had been a silly robbery. They'd have been better waiting, but rent and living on the run costs a lot. When Tony returned both men were thinking the same thing: from now on no more odd jobs. It was time for a big job.

**'A receptionist of a hotel at the Martelaarsgracht got robbed and cuffed by two men this morning. The two robbers threatened the victim with a gun and seized an unknown amount of money. The robbers managed to get away.'** *Source: Nieuws van de Dag, Tuesday 2nd April 1991*

## Chapter Eight: Chase Along The Canals

Next morning, Brendan and Tony went out in the car to get to know Amsterdam better and to look for their next target. It was a nice but necessary ride. If you don't know where to go in a city, you have a problem once the police are after you. There was plenty of traffic and a high police presence in Amsterdam. Tony drove the Opel 2000i, which they'd collected two days before, through the centre of the city. The 'tourist route' went along canals and over bridges and cobble roads. Amsterdam looked wonderful on this sunny day. Cafe owners had put their tables and chairs out on the pavement. The canals were filled with all kind of motorboats, pedal boats and water buses.

The car windows were down and the guns were well concealed along with some balaclavas, which Brendan always kept in their working cars in case of emergencies. They hadn't a clue where they were. Neither man knew the roads. The tram, bicycles and cars had their own lanes. It was a bit confusing when you weren't used to it, especially in a country where they drive on the right side of the road. As they turned into a small road and drove along, past the shops on each side, Brendan noticed the Dutch people walking there were looking into the car. He began to feel quite uncomfortable. Surely people weren't this nosey in this country?

Ahead, coming into view, were some red and white bollards. The road they were on had been closed. As they got closer Brendan could see there were two cops getting out of their police car on the other side of the bollards, paying all their attention to the Opel heading towards them. It was only then they realised they'd been driving on a road where cars weren't allowed and was pedestrianised. The cops came running towards the Opel. Tony didn't hesitate and swung the car round. There was only just enough room to turn it and speed away. All the people were stopped looking at the car and these two police running up after it.

At the end of the street they managed to get back on the normal road, but after the first corner they were met by a police car with the lights flashing. The cops were waving for them to stop. Tony nodded. It was the signal to reach down, grab the balaclavas and put them on. Grabbing the guns also, which were hidden under the dashboard, they now had to shake off the pursuers.

It wouldn't really matter if they lost the car. Like always, they were both wearing light surgical gloves, so there never would be any fingerprints to find. The car wasn't tied to anybody. The only thing that mattered was that the police didn't see theirr faces. Both men were still unknown to the Dutch police, although not to the British and Irish.

Tony was an excellent driver, especially under pressure. He was well used to be chased by the police. It was something from growing up in Ireland, where the boys from the estate would go to town on the weekend and take a car to joyride. The ultimate kick was to attract the attention of the Garda with the stolen car and provoke a pursuit. The Garda were the worst drivers in the world, but there were a lot of them. The car chases were great fun. When there were ten to fifteen cars with blue flashing lights behind, the buzz was great. If they got too close, they use to head for the estate where a permanent array of rocks and petrol bombs would give them a rude wake up call. A gallon of petrol made twelve petrol bombs.

Molotov-cocktails were like toys to the two brothers. One day Brendan had been throwing petrol bombs at a very high wall with some friends. Behind the wall was a farm. Even to this day no one is quite sure how it happened, but one of the group missed the wall and the Molotov-cocktail went over. The farmer had just bought the winter hay and, of course, the petrol bomb hit it and the farm was ablaze in seconds. Six cows were burned and the farm was gutted. It smouldered for weeks after. Every day Brendan passed it on the way to the Christian Brothers' College.

For half an hour the Amsterdam ring of canals was a dangerous place to be. In a matter of two minutes they were being chased by three or four police cars. Brendan sat back and let Tony drive. They raced along the canals and over the small humped bridges that Amsterdam has. With a lot of creativity Tony made manoeuvres alongside cars and bicycles, sometimes using the path ways. Cyclists stepped down from their bikes to have a look, pedestrians quickly made themselves scarce.

Neither Brendan or Tony had a notion which way to go. They'd not been in the city long enough to get to know the endless streets and canal routes. The Dutch police were driving little white Volkswagen Golfs. They knew the streets and were not bad drivers, but despite this Brendan had full confidence in his brother's driving and knew he'd get them out of this.

They were making a decent lead on the police cars when a man on a pushbike with a child on the back wouldn't move out of the way. He can't have failed to hear the Opel's roaring engine and the police sirens behind him, but he just ignored everything and carried on cycling along. The police were right behind now, but they still had to catch them. All they knew was there were two men in balaclavas. Eventually the guy on the bike got out of the way and they were able to speed off and put a bit of distance between the police and them.

After a few minutes of gaining ground they went over a bridge, took the first left and finally found a parking space in the long line of cars. Like something out of the Italian Job they stopped, reversed in and ducked down. Seconds later Brendan and Tony watched the police cars come racing by. They waited until they were out of sight, got out of the car and crossed the road. After turning a few corners they got off the street and went into a cafe for a cup of tea. From the window they sat at they saw a couple of police cars, looking for the Opel. Leaving the cafe they needed to find somewhere to hide for a couple of hours.

The first opportunity that presented itself was the Van Gogh Museum and they went in to have a look at the famous artist's work. Brendan couldn't believe how much these paintings were worth, but they were not marketable. He could rob them, but could hardly sell them. Art theft wasn't his thing.

After a while the coast seemed clear and Brendan and Tony got the tram and the metro, heading for Bijlmermeer, a suburb of Amsterdam containing only blocks of flats. Here they were due to meet a couple they knew from Dublin, who lived in one of these flats. During the ride the two men discussed their financial situation. They really needed to build up some money. Then they would have to keep quiet until more money was needed. They had a few thousand, but that wouldn't last long as they were still paying for the hotel rooms and two flats they'd rented out. This might be viewed as an unnecessary expense, but to Brendan it was a priority in case something unforeseen happened and they needed a safe place for the night.

On the way to Bijlmermeer, the tram went past a Dutch prison. It had high rise blocks for jails with the usual big walls surrounding it but they could still make out some prisoners in the yards. A few stops after that, in a jungle of flat blocks, they reached their destination. The friend met them at the station and took them to his flat. It was nice to see him and they chatted about years earlier in Ireland and just enjoyed the evening. The hospitality of his and his wife helped the tension flow away.

## Chapter Nine: Albert Heijn

The Bijlmermeer with its big tall blocks of flats was like an alien land-scape. The tallest buildings in Dublin were the Ballymun flats of only a few floors high. The flat where the two brothers were staying was on the eighth floor. Brendan had never been so high up. Next to the flats was the Gaasperpark. Brendan would run every morning here when he could. Often he persuaded Tony to join him. One sunny day Tony suggested to go boating on the Gaasperplas, a lake in the middle of this park. At the water sports club they hired a rowing boat. 'I'll row you. Relax', Tony said. He rowed to the middle of the lake and let the boat drift. It was a beautiful sunny day. Brendan closed his eyes and started to fantasise about a few hundred thousand pounds lying around. He knew that in any densely populated area, there always was money around somewhere. The trick was to find out where it was and how to get it.

There was no doubt about it, they needed money. There were plenty of banks and cash depots around, but it would just take time to get all the facts together and come up with a plan for taking the money.

As the boat gently rocked, Brendan could feel the hot sun on his face and he began to drift off. No sooner had his eyes closed when he was rudely awoken by several enormous bangs. It took a couple of seconds to come to and for his mind to register what was happening. Tony was standing up in the boat with a smoking gun in his hands. A family of ducks had come by the boat, only for Tony to take his piece out and shoot them. There were bits of duck everywhere. He'd almost emptied the clip. He turned around to say something, but Brendan was already rowing to the side of the lake. He was furious and shouted 'What do you think you're doing shooting fucking ducks in the middle of a fucking park?! For fucks sake!!' Tony genuinely couldn't understand why his brother was so pissed off.
'Have you gone mad? What if the police come flying in here now? I'm finding it hard to understand what the fuck all this is about!'.

Walking back to the flat Brendan let rip again: 'All the time we're being careful not to catch the eye of the police. We're changing our cars every two weeks, spending huge amounts on safe houses and ID's and checking every car parked around, for you to just get us in shit, killing fucking ducks!!' Tony heaved a deep sigh. 'Fuck, I'm fed up of just hanging around. Sorry for doing that though' he said.

The following day, calm again, Brendan went over to Albert Heijn, a big supermarket in a shopping centre in Kraaiennest. He'd picked up some stuff for breakfast. Eggs, bacon, bread and stuff and he was waiting in line to be served. It was very busy and as he waited he looked at all the other people in the other lines. There were lots of tills, as busy at it came and he wondered if it was like this all day, all week. How many of those people, waiting in line patiently led plain normal lives? At that moment Brendan would have loved to step into their shoes and just be normal. But there he was, armed with a .357 Magnum, a

Browning 9 mm semi automatic and a spare clip, a speed loader for 'Maggie'. By just buying breakfast he could get ten years or more if he was pulled now. But by now Brendan was finding it absolutely normal to be armed all the time and to obtain a new identity every couple of weeks. There was never an opportunity to get settled. He always had to move on after a couple of weeks, just to stay out of the hands of the police. In reality, he was going nowhere really, just round in a big pointless circle and it was beginning to get him down. He'd have loved to go back to the days before and not have to look over his shoulder all the time. Such is life.

Looking at the huge amount of customers and the many tills he wondered if it was busy like this all the time. There had to be plenty of money going around. Perhaps he should find out how they could get this money.

Brendan watched the supermarket open and then watched it close. It would be mostly cash. Over the next two weeks he had someone follow the manager home and to work. He was very predictable and Brendan knew he could take full advantage of this. Tony arranged the cars, the safe drop offs, the route and all other nitty-gritty things.

They decided to do it on a morning, just after 5.00 A.M. The manager always drove in and parked opposite the metal doors, behind which was an elevator that brought him to ground level. They didn't know what would happen 'alarm wise' once inside. The manager would have to pass all that on.

The manager pulled in on time, just as Brendan and Tony had observed the few times that they'd watched from across the road on a car park level. He got out and before he could realise what was happening, his arm was twisted up his back and a gun pushed in his chest. 'Go in and turn off the alarms. Do it! Then we'll speak further' Brendan ordered.

Both men were dressed in black track suits with black balaclavas. Tony carried the FN Browning 9mm, Brendan carried the 357 Magnum. They had recruited a driver, who had two more 9mm guns in the car. Under a blanket in the back there were two pumps as well.

They walked the manager over to the door of the elevator. While Tony watched the area, Brendan called the lift and then all three took the lift and went down to the ground floor. As the lift opened and they walked into the supermarket the manager was told to switch off all the alarms and explain the system. He was extremely nervous they tried to calm him down. 'You won't be harmed' Brendan said. 'All you have to do is give us the money. And when your staff arrive, you will tell them to mind their own business and not to interfere. They have to lie down and keep quiet. You'll have to repeat this to each employee'.

Brendan went back up with the manager in the lift. He put him with his back against the back wall of the lift, facing the doors and Brendan took position besides these lift doors, so the people walking in directly passed him only saw the manager to begin with. They would only notice Brendan when the doors closed behind them and the manager had finished his little speech.

Brendan had his balaclava pulled down and the Magnum held down by his side. Nobody offered any resistance. Each time he went down in the lift, Tony was waiting to take people over, leading them to the space they'd picked in the stores. Tony tied their hands behind their backs, laid them on the floor and guarded them.

After a while there was not enough space to put the bodies. Even when they moved them closer together, it was still getting tight. There were about twenty bodies down on the floor and people were still arriving. They'd been tying them up since 5.00 A.M. It was now 7.30 A.M and it was still another hour before the time lock would go off. The driver would give the signal if anything was wrong outside. All they had to do was wait and be alert.

Brendan asked the manager to ask if everyone was alright. Two people asked to use the toilet. Tony took them one at a time, brought them back and then retied them and laid them down in the aisles. This place was huge. Brendan wondered how much money the safe contained. He was hoping it was enough to be able to relax for a while.

The lift bell rang again. A big man with a beard appeared on the screen of the CCTV. It was a lorry driver who'd arrived to deliver supplies to the supermarket. Brendan went up and collected him, but they'd had run out of things to tie people up with so he got shoelaces from some of the employees to cuff the man up with. He went over to the giant fridge, went inside and closed the door. After staying in there for a few minutes he knew it wasn't too cold. They could leave the people in here once they'd got the money bagged up and were ready to go.

Some more people rang the bell and were brought in to get tied up in the fridge. Meanwhile Brendan was beginning to get things prepared for leaving. He went into the strong room with the manager, who turned out to be a very cooperative, polite Dutchman. The manager said that the time lock of the safe went off before 8.30 A.M, which sounded like good news. And it was because shortly after 8.00 A.M. the time lock clicked off. Brendan motioned the Magnum towards the safe and said: 'Open it!'

The manager used the combination dial and the other key and opened the door. 'Sit down on your hands, face the wall in the corner and close your eyes!' Brendan ordered. He obeyed. Brendan looked in the safe. It was full of these little black hard plastic boxes. He took one out and saw it contained a bundle of Dutch guilders with some kind of plastic traps across it, holding it down. Using a big sharp knife he opened the strap and the money sprung up. Brendan emptied it out. It was used 25-guilder notes. He began to pull out a few and open them, putting all the notes in the large holdall. It was soon almost full, but because of the small currencies - notes of ten guilders and so on - he decided to fill two black bin liners, doubled for strength, and just take all the boxes too. There were two big black bags full of money boxes.

Brendan signalled the manager to get up and follow. He walked over to to Tony. 'We're ready' he said.

Tony rounded the people up and then walked them all to the giant fridge and put them in. 'Don't be scared' he told the manager. 'You won't freeze to death. The police will be here soon to free you'.

The door was closed and jammed it shut. They had to get away quickly. The complex security would soon notice no activity in its biggest store. At least, that's if they hadn't noticed yet!

They'd taken the precaution of letting two women stock and restock the aisles near the big windows, just for the benefit of the complex security patrol. They'd even swapped them for two different ones half way through. The whole robbery depended on things looking normal, like always.

Brendan checked the screen. Nobody was outside so they got in the lift with the bags, pressed the lift button and went up. The doors opened and as they got out Tony pressed the button to send the lift back down. The black bin bags were awkward to carry. The two men turned right as they left and walked up towards the underground car park and into the morning sunshine. It was 8.15 A.M. They'd been in Albert Heijn around three hours. Anytime now the police would be there, trying to trace the perpetrators of the robbery.

The driver got them to the safe drop. It was a flat near an industrial estate and near a McDonald's drive-in. They got out of the car and took the bags from the boot. Tony nodded to the driver and he pulled off in the car. He would dump it after cleaning it up and then he'd collect his money in a day or two. Brendan used the key to get into the flat. The owner was there and he had a visitor. After quickly exchanging pleasantries Brendan and Tony went into the back room. There they opened all the boxes and emptied the money onto the floor. A rough estimate put it over a couple of hundred thousand guilders. There were cheques too.

They changed out of their black tracksuits and trainers and put on suits, ties and sunglasses. Then they put the money into one big briefcase and the other half into a smart small case. They'd be alright travelling alone and now looked just like businessmen. Tony then took the cable tram, which was next door to the flat more or less. Brendan walked into the industrial estate and got a taxi.

The arrangement had been to both meet downtown at the Leidseplein, in the Bulldog café. From there they would travel on to Rotterdam separately. There was already a flat and hotel room waiting there and the men would buy two new passports and adopt a new identity. This time tomorrow they could be leaving Holland and start to discover the world together. Brendan was looking forward to it; Tony was good company.

It was only recently Brendan's brother had decided to spend some time with him. The past four years on the run he'd had been mostly by himself. Tony had become Brendan's companion at the robberies. It was where all the money came from for living. There was no enjoyment in doing them. It was just business for them.

They'd talked about buying two big powerful bikes and touring around Europe for two or three months. Just to have a look round and keep their heads down.Via Rotterdam, Belgium and France they'd planned to go to Spain. Maybe the next month they could go across back into Portugal. It was too early to decide. First they had to get out of this country.

The taxi pulled into the Dam square and Brendan got out and paid. He decided to head down to the Leidseplein to meet Tony. It was early, but already the tourists were out with their cameras. It's a quite nice place, Amsterdam. It's a pity he always got into trouble there, he thought to himself.

After a nice walk Brendan arrived in the Bulldog cafe. Tony wasn't there yet so he ordered a coffee and sat down. He'd give Tony half an hour. Maybe he'd been held up for some reason. Brendan had just finished his coffee, when Tony walked in. He looked very smart in his suit. 'Can I buy you a drink?', he asked. 'Water please'. Tony ordered a coke. He sat back with his sunglasses still on, smiling with his eyebrows raised. 'What's in the briefcase?', he said. Brendan laughed. It was an old 'in' joke with a few of them from childhood Once there had been a briefcase containing £2000 in the boot of a stolen car they'd been driving. Since then they'd always joked if a briefcase was involved in anything.

'What kept you?' Brendan asked. 'I dropped in some place for a shower and shave' Tony said. Neither had eaten a thing since the early evening before and were starving. Three men, who'd walked in a few minutes earlier were laughing at the counter. Two of them took out their shades, put them on and looked over at Tony grinning. 'Do you think they'd find it funny if I just shot the three of them?' Tony asked smiling. Brendan laughed. 'Come on. We have better things to do. Maybe the next stranger they are rude to will put some manners on them'.

The two men moved onto a restaurant nearby, had a meal and said goodbye. 'I'll see you in Rotterdam' Brendan said. 'You go by train; I'll get a taxi'. The Amsterdam cab driver nearly gave himself a hernia lifting Brendan's case. 'What the hell is in it?' he gasped with exhaustion. 'Money and weapons' he answered. The man laughed. So did Brendan.

Once they'd arrived in Rotterdam Brendan had to pay him the fare, which was 150 guilders. He didn't have the money in his wallet, so he had to open the case. The driver didn't get a glimpse in it and was quite astonished when Brendan grabbed some banknotes out of the case without even looking in it.

In the Rotterdam hotel room, which they had rented with a false name, Brendan waited for Tony. As time passed he was beginning to get a bit annoyed by this, because they had many things to do. They had to sort out all the money properly and collect two passports. The current passports they were using were from the same source. They were expensive but worth it.

After a long wait, when Tony still hadn't shown up, Brendan left the hotel and spent the night with a girl, who lived in a flat down to the docks of

Rotterdam. He just hoped nothing had happened to Tony.

**'Two armed men robbed a branch of Albert Heijn in the Kraaiennest Shopping Centre (South-East Amsterdam) yesterday. The couple threatened the employees of the supermarket with a firearm and left with an unknown amount of money. No one got injured during the robbery.'**
*Source: De Telegraaf, Friday 31st May 1991*

# Chapter Ten: Tramlijn 12

As Brendan paid the taxi driver, got out and took a slow walk up the road he looked at all the parked cars and in the reflection of the shop-windows he checked if he was being followed. He was feeling a little annoyed at having to come back to Amsterdam. It was the day after the Albert Heijn robbery. Tony was supposed to come to Rotterdam, but hadn't shown up. By now they should have already left Holland. Brendan didn't like travelling through Amsterdam and Tony knew it. This city had become too hot for them.

Tony had phoned that morning and asked him to have dinner with him and his girlfriend, Sarah. Brendan didn't like it, but he agreed. The restaurant was in the middle of the street. He walked up to the top of the road and back down and when he didn't see anyone suspicious he walked into the restaurant. Tony and the girl were sitting at the back and Brendan noticed a quite bulky plastic bag at his brothers feet. As he sat down, the girl said: 'Okay, now we can eat'. It would take at least another hour before he could talk freely with Tony so they made conversation, had a meal, ordered coffee, paid the bill and eventually left the place.

'What's in the bag, Tony?' asked Brendan in a low voice. 'A hundred thousand guilders and two handguns', Tony answered. Now Brendan was even more annoyed. Instead of taking his loot to the safe house in Rotterdam he'd just taken his share to the restaurant.

Outside a tram was coming, heading towards Central Station. Brendan suggested that he and Tony get on it, put the girl in a cab and eventually go to Rotterdam by themselves. As they were standing waiting at the tram stop, they could hear the sound of sirens. The police were busy with some nearby commotion. The tram arrived and all three got in. It was full, except for a few seats at the end.

As the tram travelled to the next stop, the police sirens seemed to be staying with the tram. They decided to purchase three tickets for the tram, as sometimes ticket inspectors get on and check. They could do without the extra attention. As Brendan went to the front of the tram to pay, the police sirens were getting louder. On the road parallel to the tram tracks he glimpsed blue lights flashing on the walls of the lanes that led through to the next streets. Looking back he could see Tony and Sarah talking at the back of the tram. Behind them, through the rear window of the tram, he could see blue lights on the bend of the road. As Brendan got close to the driver he noticed he was in the middle of an agitated conversation on his radio.

The tram approached the next stop. After the doors opened, Brendan noticed a man standing there, just looking at him. He looked odd and didn't try to get on the tram. At that moment he knew something was very wrong and in a flash put a gun to the driver's head. 'Lock the doors and put the radio down!' Brendan shouted. 'Tony! Police!' Tony was on his feet, squeezing himself to the front through the crowd of people.

They were being surrounded. Brendan couldn't believe it. All the effort he put in to avoid things exactly like this. For four years they'd been extremely careful not to get into trouble. He'd always made sure everything was meticulously planned with a plan B always in place. Just one day before they'd dumped their cars, with the intention of never coming back to Amsterdam. And now here they were, being surrounded on a fucking tram, in downtown Amsterdam. He never should have gone to that restaurant.

Taking control of the situation Brendan told everyone to stand up and face the window. For the benefit of those who didn't speak English, he motioned with the gun and was understood. 'Put the tram into reverse and move it!' he told the driver. He moved some levers, but nothing happened. The man tried again: nothing. 'They've turned off the electricity' he explained. They were stuck as could be in the middle of the Ferdinand Bolstraat, a main road in De Pijp, an old part of Amsterdam. The police seemed to be everywhere.

Tony looked towards Brendan and mouthed the word 'sorry'. 'What's happened?' Tony answered: 'I dropped into the Irish couple. I wanted to thank them for their hospitality and give them some money'. It was the most naïve thing he could have done. Less than 24 hours after the armed robbery Tony had visited the former safe house, just around the corner of Albert Heijn. The police, of course, had already found out the house had been used by the perpetrators of the robbery and they must have followed Tony, way before he walked into the restaurant. Brendan knew it and he could tell by Tony's eyes he did too. 'It doesn't matter now what way they come at us. All that counts is our next step' Brendan emphasised.

Escaping from this situation wouldn't be easy. The tram was full of people. Maybe they could work it out to get off with the hostages. At least one of them could slip away like that. 'What do you think of the situation?' Brendan asked. Tony summed it up in a nut shell: 'The three of us are stuck in a glass carriage, in the middle of a main road, fully surrounded and we've got two guns. We won't get away'.

Outside nothing was happening, apart from blue lights reflecting and lightening up the night. 'What do you think of Amsterdam now, Bren?' Tony asked with a cheerful voice. In serious situations Tony always came out with funny, surprising things and it made Brendan laugh.

The tram passengers were getting apprehensive. 'Why are you keeping us here?' one of them asked. His face was a mix of fear and anger. Brendan, slightly taken aback by his cheek answered 'Don't worry and don't speak again!' Once one started and got away with it, the rest of the people would sense the mood. It was already happenening. Some of the passengers who had previously been just looking out of the windows were turning to look. It was then Brendan knew they were not going anywhere on this one. It was important to keep all the passengers facing the windows, so that it would be too risky for the police to shoot.

Looking at Tony, Brendan wished he could put him somewhere safe away from this. The police were all around the tram with their guns pointing at them. 'It doesn't look good' he said. 'The best we can do now is lessen the damage'. He continued: 'I'm on the run anyway, Tony. I want you to walk out with all passengers and try to get away. I'll stay here.

'Bren, I think I brought them to the restaurant. They already know my face and yours. For me it doesn't make sense to run away. I say we let them all go. Sarah can go with them and take our things with her on the way off'.

'I agree Tony'. Brendan looked over at Sarah and winked. 'You'll be alright' in the friendliest way he could. Inwardly his blood was boiling. He'd only come here because this little madam asked Tony to go for a meal.

Sarah was scared and shaking as they told her what to do. 'And what should I do with the bag?' she blubbered. Brendan told her to put it in a house they both knew. She nodded a yes. He pushed a small note in the palm of her hand and said: 'Contact this number'. It was the number of a solicitor who had a good reputation. A contact in Amsterdam had recommended him and Brendan and Tony had previously agreed to use this lawyer if need be, and this was the time. In a few moments they would let all the hostages go, put the guns and money in the bag. Sarah could take the bag with her and then there would be only Tony and Brendan. Tony would be alright. He wasn't wanted but Brendan was already an escaper. He'd been one for four years.

The police had not tried to contact them in almost an hour so the to men decided to just chat till they let the people go. 'What do you have in mind?' Tony asked. 'Well, we will be going to different jails. I think we should use it as a rest and have a break to think things out'. Everything in Holland was at an end. One flat in Amsterdam, one in Rotterdam, both in nice areas, four rooms in different hotels, cars; everything had already been shut down. The arrangements to leave had all been made. The only thing to do now was go to jail, recuperate, escape and leave Holland, a bit later than planned. Tony agreed, they were both tired and could do with a rest.

For Brendan, this was a bad moment and he didn't like it one bit. They would be separated and if they had their way, he wouldn't see Tony for two years. He was one of the very few people he trusted one hundred percent.

Before they let the hostages go Brendan and Tony needed to work out how they were going to get Sarah off the tram with the bag, without the police suspecting she was with them. A couple of girls were picked out, including Sarah. 'Listen very carefully' Brendan said to the girls. 'We're about to let you go. We'll give you a phone number, which you have to call. If it's answered, just tell the person two people are arrested for something they don't know anything about. Tell him we are Irish, but non-political.' The number was the for the solicitor. The girls said they would do it.

Brendan and Tony stripped down their clothes to show they were unarmed. They didn't know what the police in Holland were like. They shook hands and hugged. Each hoped the other would be alright. 'Keep in touch when you can' Tony said. Brendan smiled, turned to face the hostages and said: 'Right, let's go!'

The driver opened the door and was first off the tram. Everyone else moved quickly to the door. Everyone seemed to be out for themselves and Brendan was surprised to see some of the men pushing their way in front of the women. That's just the way they all felt: get away. He would understand that phrase so very well himself in the years ahead.

The last few people went out of the door, leaving Brendan and Tony sitting in the middle of the tram with their hands on the rail in front of them, to show they had no weapons. People were running away from the tram and the police were moving them away. Other policemen were coming into the doorway, shouting in Dutch to each other. A few moments later a Dutch cop was pointing a gun at them, then another and more were taking up positions. 'Show your hands!' they shouted as they approached. Soon Brendan and Tony were handcuffed. They didn't answer anything they were asked. As they were led from the tram to a waiting vehicle Brendan noticed the plastic bag Sarah was supposed to take with her was still there. He never heard from her again.

At the police station they took finger prints and the two men were put in separate cells. It was late evening and Brendan lay down on the cell bed and closed his eyes.

**'By arresting two Irish brothers, the Amsterdam police solved the robbery of a supermarket at Kraaiennest on Thursday last week. During the robbery fifteen employees were locked in a fridge. The suspects are the 28 years old B.Q and the 30 years old A.Q.**
**The two men were arrested in tram 12, after they threatened the driver with a firearm. They could see they were being chased and wanted to use the tram to shake off the police. The driver saw a chance to give alarm. Policemen entered the carriage in the Ferdinand Bolstraat. About 25 passengers left the tram quickly. Both men stripped the upper part of their bodies to show they were unarmed.**
**The suspects appeared to carry the loot of last week's robbery with them. Some tens of thousands of guilders are involved. Also, two firearms were confiscated by the police.**
**Police investigations showed that the two brothers had been living in South East Amsterdam for months, while on the run for the British authorities. The 28 years old suspect escaped from prison in 1988, where he was being held after several robberies. Also, his brother was wanted for several robberies.'**
*Source: De Telegraaf, Tuesday 4th June 1991.*

After a couple of days in the police cell Brendan found himself caught up in an astonishing incident. In the interview room an attaché-case was thrown on the table. 'Do you know this case?' Yes, of course he knew it. It was the one he'd left behind in the girl's flat in Rotterdam, where he'd spent the night after the robbery on Albert Heijn. He'd put 30,000 guilders in it, and a handgun on top of the money. He'd arranged to pick up the case later. But how the hell did they find it? One of the investigators turned the front of the case towards Brendan. 'We failed to open it. We'd like to ask you if you can do this for us. I guess you know the combination of the lock'.

With a penetrating gaze the investigator bent over the table. Brendan felt something was wrong, but decided to unlock the case. Flipping the locks open with two thumbs, with a quick move he lifted the lid and tried to grab the handgun. The case was empty. It was an embarrassing moment. The detective just watched his reaction and then left the room.

The police found the safe house in Rotterdam with good old fashioned detective work. During his arrest on the tram Brendan had a bunch of six keys. The investigators went to a locksmith, who was able to tell in which areas this kind of keys was used. The investigation led to the block of flats in Rotterdam, where all the locks were tried, until they found the right address.

From the police station in Amsterdam Brendan was transported to the Bijlmerbajes-prison. With his hands cuffed behind his back, he was sitting in the backseat of the Volkswagen Golf. Without attracting the attention of the two cops in front, he managed to squeeze a leg through his cuffed arms. The other leg would follow any second now. As soon as he had these cuffs in front of him, the two policemen wouldn't have a chance. He would grab the driver by the throat with the cuffs. The passenger would only be able to pull his gun with his right hand. When he turned to the left to point the gun at him, Brendan would grab and twist his wrist outwards, which would make him release the gun automatically. Brendan would then have overcome both men and would be in control.

Just as he tried to get his other leg between his cuffed wrists, the driver hit the brakes and called for back up. Within a minute, they were surrounded by police cars. There he was, sitting like a little child, with his wrists between his legs. It was Brendan's second embarrassing incident in a couple of days.

## Chapter Eleven: In Court

When Brendan and Tony had to appear in court, they weren't interested in the case itself. Actually, Brendan couldn't really give a fuck what the judge was saying. For them it was just an opportunity to talk between themselves. He knew they would get no favours, no matter if they were obediently paying attention or not. If Tony hadn't been there, Brendan probably wouldn't have even bothered going to court to listen to all the bollocks they talk. Judges shouldn't be allowed to pass long sentences until they've done a mandatory term of four years in the block at one of the countries shithole prisons, without any privileges. Only then they would know what they're talking about. A judge can never imagine a life like that.

In advance of the court appearances, the special squad kept Brendan and Tony seperately in the cells downstairs. When it was time to show up, they were brought up to the court. There they could meet and talk.

The Dutch court to Brendan seemed very different to what he was used to. In the so called meervoudige strafkamer – the multiple criminal division - there are three judges, not just one. To him they all came across as very arrogant. Tony and Brendan chatted away during the trial for the robberies on Albert Heijn and the hotel. While the judge went on about all this type of stuff Brendan was telling his brother about the way they were keeping him, with lots of security. He emphasised to Tony not to bring any heat by trying to escape. 'Just sit back and relax. I'll escape first and then I'll break you out.' Tony answered relaxed: 'No problem'. Tony would arrange through the visits to get all their things in one place, preferably in the flat in Amsterdam. His visits were less secure than Brendans, so he could arrange it much more easily. They'd bought a fair few weapons from a man just over the Belgium border and Brendan was keen to collect them for easy access.

During the court appearances Brendan never spoke to anyone except Tony. So the court was quite surprised when he suddenly stood up from the court seat and put his hand up. 'Well well, Mr. Quinn. You're showing you aren't just a machine. Do you finally want to speak up?' one of the judges asked. Brendan smiled and said: 'Yes. I'd like to have a piss, judge!'

**'Because of two shameless armed robberies on an Amsterdam hotel and an Albert Heijn supermarket, the public prosecutor yesterday demanded eight years imprisonment against the Irish brothers Anthony (30) and Brendan (28) Q.**
**Both men were arrested in a tram in the Ferdinand Bolstraat on May 31, one day after the robbery on Albert Heijn. (...) They were caught carrying a revolver and 50,000 guilders of the stolen amount of 150,000 guilders.**
**On April 2nd the Quinn brothers, from whom the youngest escaped in England from remand, entered hotel Astoria at the Martelaarsgracht. They**

surprised the owner, who resisted severely. Eventually they managed to tie the woman down to hands and feet and make her tell the combination of the safe. They took away 10,000 guilders, some wristwatches and golden jewels. They left with the words: 'Don't go to the police, or we'll kill you'.

At the Albert Heijn supermarket at Kraaiennest Anthony and Brendan forced all fifteen employees to enter the canteen by putting guns against their heads. The people had to lie down on their belly. One of the employees was put into action as a translator. He had to put over that nobody would get hurt and nobody should interfere, because the money wasn't theirs anyway. The manager was forced to lead them to the safe, where the time lock went off once they got there. The loot was disappointing to the brothers. They had expected double the amount.

The prosecutor, who believes that the Qs came to their action under the influence of drugs, criticised their indifference in respect of their victims. 'The death threat was very real for everyone. This kind of robbery has a tremendously traumatic effect on people. Albert Heijn has put a special trauma team into action, which unfortunately has its hands full with the employees.

Verdict: 14th October.

*Source: De Telegraaf, Tuesday 1st October 1991*

On 14th October 1991 Brendan and Tony were found guilty of the robberies and sentenced to six years imprisonment. The public prosecutor had demanded eight years. The judge also ordered that Brendan had to give back the amount of 1800 guilders which he'd carried with him during one of the robberies. Of course, he never handed over the money and they appealed to the Gerechtshof, but this higher court brought in the same verdict.

Brendan didn't really care. All he was interested in was escaping and getting more money. And that was going to happen. Exactly three months after the verdict he broke out of De Geerhorst in Sittard. Three months after that he committed the robbery on the C1000 supermarket in North Amsterdam.

## Chapter Twelve: Young and Armed

A screw opened the door, poked his head in and said: 'Mr. Quinn, they are coming for you in ten minutes'. It was 7.00 A.M. and still quiet on the unit. Two and half months had gone by now since the robbery on C1000. Brendan was to be moved from De Grittenborgh-prison in Hoogeveen to another EBI.

The EBI-unit in Hoogeveen was similar to the one in Sittard. There were just different faces, but more or less all of the screws had one and the same agenda. They all psychologically fucked around with your head and seemed to only be happy doing this.

Every six months maximum security prisoners were moved from one EBI to another. With this merry-go-round the Dutch Justice Ministry thought they'd put a stop to escapes or liberations. Brendan didn't know why they'd moved him already. They either knew something or were suspicious. It had to be one way or the other. For now, he had to leave every thought of an escape from Hoogeveen, but maybe in the future he'd be back.

He had now visited two of the four EBIs in Holland. In the reception the special squad were waiting. Being as cautious as ever they placed a black hood over his head and after the usual tedious security procedures, they were on their way out of Hoogeveen. Brendan assumed they would take him to De Schie in Rotterdam or De Marwei in Leeuwarden.

During the ride he weighed up his options. If he played along with the prison system, how long would he have to wait to go to a lower security jail? More than likely it would be years. A part of him was just unable to accept that. His only option was to escape.

It's what Brendan spent most of his time looking for, just a way out. Just a mistake or something overlooked could be enough to attempt an escape. The question however presented itself where would he go. His heart was in Ireland, but going back to his home patch was out of the question. Because of his criminal history in Ireland and his escape from the London prison, Brendan knew he would be hunted constantly. Actually, it had been the story of his life. From his youngest years in Dublin Brendan had been on the run.

He'd been only fifteen years old when he was accused of his first armed robbery. The Garda raided the family home early one morning and took him off to the station. They claimed Brendan had held up a mini market in Dundrum the previous day. The owner and assistant had been putting the week's wages in a car when another car pulled up. Two men had jumped out: one with a sawn-off shotgun, the other with an iron bar. After forcing the two men to lie down on the floor they had taken the money. Their getaway car had been blocked with a bus, crammed with people as they were about to drive off. So one person had got back out of the car, walked over to the bus driver and presented him a choice: move the bus or be shot. Apparently, the driver realised what an idiot he was and reversed off the pathway into a load of traffic. The gunmen had got back in the car and sped off.

Brendan had been taken to an interrogation room, where six detectives tried to bully him into making a statement. He didn't say anything to them and was charged, but he got out on bail because he'd only been fifteen years old. The three older boys who were also accused with Brendan had been charged too, but they all made statements. During the trial the three of them admitted everything, while Brendan refused to speak. 'They're all lying. I wasn't there' he told his lawyer. The three older boys received two years each. Brendan was found not guilty. He didn't speak to any of the three of them again, even though one of them had been his cousin.

Brendan's parents had been very upset when he'd been arrested for such a thing. He juist told them that he didn't know why they'd accused him of such a serious crime. After this, Brendan's father decided to get the boys off the street. He bought a van, insured it and got Brendan and Tony jobs delivering down the country. It was great work and good wages, till they were sacked. One day they'd got a blow out in Kildare and the paperwork had got mixed up. They ended up delivering the wrong things to Limerick and Galway. They were delivering coal then, but the money wasn't worth it and the work fizzled out too.

The Garda had been harassing Brendan since he'd been arrested and acquitted on the armed robbery. They felt he'd got away with it unscathed. Sometimes their car was stopped six times a day. Often, he was brought in and held for two days under section 30: 'offences against the state'. After being released at the back of the Garda station, he would then be arrested on the same section 30. Then they would take him to another station for two days. It was a pain in the arse.

One day Brendan and Tony were stopped and arrested in Rathmines. They were brought to the Garda station, put in a cell and just left there for two days. They had learned from the beginning not to waste their time asking them anything, not even their names, nothing. That evening, as they lay down in the cell, Brendan noticed a sheet of thick plywood at the ceiling. On further examination he found it could be raised up. Both of them went up onto the cell ceiling and crawled along the rafters. Through a gap they could see these big lunatic Garda using type writers - one handed, a letter a minute. They worked their way to the end of the attic and got out through the tiled roof, escaping into the night.

Eventually Brendan got convicted for armed robbery. He was about eighteen years old when, with his uncle, he started looking at Chadwicks, a store for builder's supplies. They'd got information that the three office workers of Chadwicks always collected the wages on Thursday. There would be roughly £25,000.

The offices where they would bring the wages were to the right of the car park. Brendan and his uncle waved to the security guard who opened the barrier and they simply drove in. Parking the car down by the offices they observed the three office workers collecting the money. As the three of them pulled in the balaclavas came down and the two men got out of the car. One of the office workers saw them approaching and ran away. He was holding two money pouches. Brendan fell in behind him at a sprint. 'Drop it or be shot!' he shouted. It had the desired effect and the man dropped the money. Brendan picked it up and sprinted back to the car. By the time he arrived his uncle had three or four people lying on the floor with his foot on the chest of one man lying down, with the piece pointing at his head. Brendan ran over to the car and spun it round to pick up his uncle. At the security barrier he pointed something at the guard and motioned 'raise the barrier!'. He did.

They went to a safe house, about two miles from the robbery. When they entered the house, it turned out there had been a leak somewhere. It wasn't long though before the Garda completely surrounded the house with guns drawn. Neither Brendan or his uncle had any idea at the time who had informed the police. One year later it would come to light which little scumbag had betrayed them.

They were charged and put into custody. One of the detectives liked to play his favourite game: Russian roulette. Today Brendan was the target. He used a .38 revolver and pulled the trigger a few times. Brendan looked at him and thought: 'Cop yourself on ye halfwit. Nobody is impressed'.

It didn't do their case any good when it emerged that both of Brendan's uncles were previously convicted for IRA membership. Jumping on this, they tried to convict them on fund raising for the Republican Movement. Brendan didn't even know anyone who was in the IRA. Nobody in the IRA broadcasts to anyone that they are members, so how is anyone to know about it?

The two men were convicted in Dublin High Court, after successfully arguing the case should not go to the special criminal court. They received four years each. After two years and four months Brendan was released.

## Chapter Thirteen: Unexpected High Punishment

As the hood was taken off his head Brendan heard someone say 'Welcome in De Schie, Mr. Quinn' While he tried to get used to the light and looked around he could see the EBI-unit was similar to the ones in Sittard and Hoogeveen. The only difference was this prison being three stores high. The EBI-unit was on the top floor.

The unit was filled with cameras. Screws were watching on each door. Sometimes it was really frustrating to see them not slipping up with the security. The unit looked too secure. Nobody could get in, like in Sittard. They were too encased into the prison. To get in or out there were too many doors to go through. Police guards surrounded the prison and just going to the yard for air involved going through seven doors and using the lift. Each door had to be opened and locked behind. This jail looked almost impossible to escape from. Brendan needed outside help, but the visits were behind glass and a screw sat there watching. Every move you made and every word you even whispered was recorded.

Also, this EBI-unit accommodated four people: besides Brendan there were two Dutch guys and a Moroccan on the unit. He was friendly and sociable with them, but mostly he did his own thing. The Moroccan, Mohammed M., was doing twenty years for shooting a bank manager on a robbery attempt. The two Dutchmen were in for drugs supply. Most prisoners on the EBI were sentenced due to drug related cases. The Dutch prisoners always seemed better off than the foreign prisoners. That was true in terms of the length of the sentence and their treatment in prison.

Going out for his regulation daily air Brendan had to use a lift to go down to the bottom floor. All the standard security measures applied. All other prisoners were on lock down. Along with the others in his unit he was also allowed out of the cell for an hour to go to a work room. This involved putting plastic clips together. It was utterly mind numbing work. The only reason they did it was to get out for an hour. Twice a week they had gym in a large cell on the unit. Also, every second evening they were allowed an hour and a half in the television room.

During his stay in De Schie Brendan recieved an unexpectedly high further sentence because of the robbery on C1000 in Amsterdam: ten years. The prosecutor had demanded sixteen years but eventually the judgment was reduced to nine years on appeal. The punishment was added on the previous sentence he had to serve for the robberies on the hotel and Albert Heijn.

**'Has anybody got killed?', British Brendan Q. (29) injured asked his lawyer yesterday, as the prosecutor demanded sixteen years imprisonment against him.**
**Apparently, he had no strong feelings about the raid on the C1000-super-market in North-Amsterdam, where he and his two accomplices controlled**

about fifteen employees for three hours in the early morning of 21 April.
'I had my hand in the biscuit tin when my mum came by', was Q's explanation of the frightening incident. But prosecutor Madam J.F. Dekking
described him without any doubt as a 'very heavy, rock-hard, completely
merciless criminal'.
Against the fellow suspects Thomas C. (37) and Colin J. (29) she demanded ten years imprisonment. These relatively heavy punishments result
from the intention of the justice administration to charge attackers, if
possible, also with kidnapping.
The raiders were in early action on the Buikslotermeerplein. After a night
in a cafe in the red-light district they were noticed in the supermarket
around 6.00 A.M.
Employees had guns put against their heads and were forced to lie down
near the cold stores in the stockroom. The victims were literally piled up
like roof-tiles, for easy reference.
(...) Brendan Q. was the leader of the gang. He is considered so dangerous that very heavy security measures were taken yesterday: policemen
in bullet-proof vests and a security gate to trace weapons. In January Q.
fled from prison in Sittard. He was already sentenced to six years due
to another robbery, together with his brother. In 1984 he got four years
imprisonment for a robbery which brought up £80,000. He also escaped
from there.
To illustrate the harrowing situation during the raid, the prosecutor gave
special attention to the fourteen-year-old Wendy, daughter of a cake
supplier, who had on her Easter holidays joined her father by way of a day
out. 'Imagine you're fourteen, and then undergo a drama like that...'
Only when it was clear to the robbers they wouldn't get a getaway car or a
helicopter and that they had no single way out, did they surrender.
Brendan Q. has remained extremely silent and his accomplices are obviously mortally afraid for him. They refused to talk about his role.
Eventually the stolen money, also from the tills, was thrown around and
more or less divided among those present. An amount of 3,300 guilders
has vanished.'
Judgment: 31 August.
*Source: De Telegraaf, Tuesday 18th August 1992.*

'Both British men made it clear they were terrified of the Irishmen. They
explained in detail about their part in the robbery, but kept their mouths
shut when the role of Brendan Q. came up. According to the police the
sturdy raider never spoke more than two sentences. 'I carried out the raid
because of a lack of money'. And after hearing the demand of the prosecutor, he smiled to his lawyer: 'Ask the prosecutor if anybody got killed?'
(...) Brendan Q, according to the prosecutor a 'very hard, completely

merciless criminal', didn't show any regret. Some people found it exciting, he thought.'
*Source: Algemeen Dagblad, Tuesday 18th August 1992*

One day Brendan was looking out of the window onto the yard and he saw Colin, his co-defendant. It wasn't possible to speak to him, but he looked up and waved. Brendan waved back and smiled. Colin wasn't a bad fellow. He was surprised he was on the normal jail wing though. Colin and Chap both got seven years, after a demand of ten years. Brendan had expected Colin would have been in the unit. The three men had created quite a stir in Holland. (appendix 1 and 2).

'The Irishman and two British men who raided a store of C1000 and threatened fifteen employees for hours in April in North-Amsterdam, were convicted yesterday to ten and seven years imprisonment.
The highest punishment was imposed on the 29 years old Brendan Q, who was the leader of the trio and had already been sentenced to heavy punishments. The court speaks in the verdict of very serious criminal offences. 'It's expected that the victims will experience long-lasting psychical consequences, on which the court also considers that the raid took place at the workplace of the employees.'
*Source: De Telegraaf, Tuesday 1st September 1992.*

## Chapter Fourteen: Escape Route From De Schie

Brendan had got information from Ruben Londoño about two bent screws working in Rotterdam De Schie, both on the extra secured department. He had their physical descriptions and would know them when he saw them. He had enough to approach them with but one of them was expensive. He asked for too much money, but of course he was in the position to do so. Now he had someone to bribe, Brendan had to start planning from scratch. It was no use approaching the screw if he had nothing for him to do.

First, he had to find a way out and then try to get the screw involved in the plan. Maybe he could deliver some keys, a gun or just some information. The only information Brendan already had were his own observations from within the unit. The routine on the wing was monotonous.

One day Brendan's lawyer came on a pre-arranged visit. He took a long shower, got ready and a few minutes later was called to the unit exit. Brendan took the big case folder with the legal papers with him and at the unit exit the screws searched him and then they were off. After three doors they arrived in the corridor. At the end of it was a walk through metal detector. Just before he went through it, he passed the legal papers to the screw as it had two metal rings through it. After taking it through the detector the screw handed it back. Brendan had spotted the first weak point: He could carry a weapon in the legal book.

Brendan concentrated on the walk to his lawyer. It could be his escape route. After the lift brought him to the ground floor, he had to go through another set of doors overlooked by two screws. Behind these doors was a corridor that ended in another door, manned by two screws that used a key to let him through. Inside were two flights of stairs and then another door, with more screws waiting. There, Brendan was told to strip off. After this search he was led into a small visiting room and locked in. The whole walk from the unit to here had taken five to six minutes.

Being so close to the main prison gates was for Brendan like being at sea for a long time and finally spotting land. Freedom is so valuable; you only know this when you have lost it.

One evening in the recreation room he noticed the bent screw talking to a colleague. There could be no mistake: this was the man. Ruben, who described the guy, was very accurate with details. Thanks to Ruben, Brendan had something in reserve. He knew this screw had taken 75,000 guilders for an escape attempt. He had pocketed it for free, because the prisoner had moved to another jail before he could try to break out. A few minutes later Brendan walked to his cell and waited for the bent screw to walk by. As he did, Brendan called his name and he came over. Brendan told him 'I won't talk about these 75,000 guilders you took. Forget it, you can keep it. But there's another 75,000 guilders up front if you want to do something for me'.

He was a little nervous and in no time it became clear to him that Brendan knew the man that had a bone to pick with him because of this previous job. But he got even more tense when Brendan told him where he collected the money from before. It was from a brothel in Rotterdam, where he also stayed all night free of charge. Brendan even knew times and dates. The amazed screw simply had no choice.

'What do you want me to do?' he asked.

'Three things. First tell me anything you think I should know, answer any questions I have and lastly bring a package up for me from my co-defendant Colin'.

'When do I get my money?'

'In exactly two weeks from now, at the same place you collected it before'.

Well, unsurprisingly the screw agreed. If he hadn't Brendan would have had no problem in telling him his boss would receive a video with him taking the money and staying in the brothel, snorting cocaine and using two hookers. Fortunately, this option wasn't necessary.

After a couple of months in De Schie things were coming together and it looked like Brendan had a pretty decent way to get out. One of the weak spots in the security was the visiting procedure. In every other prison the visitor has to report himself before being escorted to the visit room. In De Schie the prisoner was just taken to the visit room to have a look if anyone had arrived for him. You got half the escape for free!

Colin had ordered a television with a handgun made into it. He would give it directly to the bent screw or in a sealed box to Brendan's lawyer during the visiting hour. Brendan could put the gun in the legal book and go as far as the doors, next to the visiting area. Then he could take the gun out, fire a warning shot and get through the doors as quickly as possible, taking a screw with him.

But still there was a lot of thinking to do. A lot of doors were electronically opened. The slush doors before the main prison entrance doors worried him. If the screws decided not to open the second door after the first door locked, he'd be effectively trapped. That would be quite a risk.

The window from the exercise yard offered a view on the buzzer onto the slush doors. Whenever Brendan had the opportunity during exercise, he studied the behaviour of the screws. Each time he watched them pressing the buzzer, he started to count. It took them twenty seconds at most to pass the slush. Added to the rest of the escape route, it theoretically meant there would be one and a half minutes to escape. This appealed to him. The screws could do most of the escape. Brendan just had to jump them near the last few doors.

He was beginning to feel better. While he knew there would be problems living on the run, he'd rather face them than just spend years between four walls. He was 28 years old and wasn't going to do sit and do nothing about this.

The bent screw had told Colin to put in a form for the TV. Colin had agreed but just to be sure that he wasn't being tricked he sent the screw back to ask Brendan the name of his girlfriend's mother. His answer would be the proof it was okay. Because of her character, Colin and Brendan called her the terminator as a joke. With these little codes they were building up a very feasible escape plan.

One evening a young woman screw came up to the unit. A pretty girl and she knew it. She often came up for no better reason than to hang round the recreation room to chatter. This night she was talking to Mohammed the Moroccan. He was always talking to the woman screws. But this time the conversation caught Brendan's attention. It covered previous trouble in the prison. He heard the girl say: 'Imagine someone puts a gun to your head or a knife to your throat, there would be no choice but to do what they want'. It was the way she said it that caught his attention. It sounded like it was policy. Brendan pretended to have not noticed and asked her about some form or other, just to change the subject. The conversation then moved onto a lighter subject: astrology.

That night in his cell Brendan was tossing and turning and couldn't fall asleep. Her words kept popping up in his mind. He decided to ask the bent screw about the policy of escapes. When he came on duty, Brendan gave him a wink as a signal to go see him before bang up. It wasn't always easy talking on the unit. There were too many eyes watching. When he had the chance he asked him what would happen if someone had a gun or blade. He said in such a situation there would be made a distinction between regular prisoners and EBI prisoners. If it was an EBI prisoner they would do as they were told for sure.

Brendan was more or less ready to go. All he would need was some transport outside and a route to a safe house. The location of the prison was quite isolated and so he knew he'd still be miles away from anywhere once he got out. The drive was a single track road out of the jail grounds, along the river. It was too long, so for that reason he wanted to buy a small speed boat. After leaving the prison he could jump straight in the boat and cut across the river. It was a much safer way than going by car.

There was this really nice French girl working in the library. Once in a while she appeared in the unit to collect and bring books. Brendan took a chance with her one day and asked her to get him a road atlas for Rotterdam. It was a risk, because she just could report this request to the prison. She knew that as well.

A few days later Brendan was just back in his cell after taking a shower, when the door was pushed open. It was the French girl. The risk seemed to have paid off and she seemed to want to help. She said: 'Here's the book you asked for' and there was the road map of Rotterdam. As Brendan took it, he flinched. He'd pulled a muscle in his right shoulder in the gym. 'What's wrong?' she asked concerned. She sat down and started rubbing his shoulder and Brendan closed his eyes. It felt a lot better, her doing that.

Just as she was doing it, the door was pushed open. In the doorway

Brendan just before jail

Tony in jail

The wall that was jumped at Pentonville Jail

Ladders to freedom at the Sittard SSU

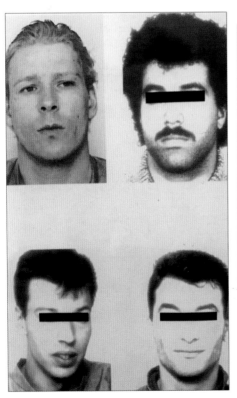

Photos used by newspapers after
Sittard escape. Brendan (top left)

Brendan's Ma and Da, with his son

A bad day at the office

The siege as it unfolded. Top left: Brendan, tooled up negotiates with cop.
Bottom left: The end of the siege. Top right: Brendan, hooded is arrested.
Bottom right: How the newspaper reported the siege.

Brendan and his Da at Frankland Jail

Above: Brendan's Da and his sister
at her wedding

Right: Brendan's son and other
relatives in the Dublin mountains

was this monstrous woman screw. 'What are you doing inside this cell?' she
shouted. 'You know the rules! Get out! I'll report you!'
The French girl left without a word. Brendan was speechless too. The girl was
very feminine and friendly, in contrast this woman screw was very horrible
and bitter. She was huge and had a hump on her back. 'What was going on
in here?' she asked. 'My shoulder is sore and the girl was just rubbing it' he
answered.

To his utter surprise and abomination this nasty woman closed the
door and started rubbing Brendan's shoulder. 'I know exactly what to do,
because of my back' she said. Brendan just sat still with the hunchback
massaging his shoulder, still not quite believing what was happening. After
a minute or two had passed he couldn't take it any longer. This had to stop.
Standing up, he thought fast and annouced: 'I have to get dressed. My lawyer
will be arriving any moment now'. She growled something and left. Brendan was
left wondering if the Dutch government had purposely trawled the land looking
for the ugliest and bitterest woman they could find, just to make criminals think
twice about committing another crime.

The bent screw in De Schie had looked a bit anxious as he told Brendan he'd just attended a security meeting. 'They will move you to another prison
in two weeks time. You're considered an incorrigible escaper and therefore a
high risk. So, they move you from EBI to EBI regularly. We're told to be extra
alert until you're moved'. This announcement put extra pressure on. Brendan
had to escape as quick as possible and told the screw everything needed to be
sped up. They must have got wind of something.

Over the next few days things started falling apart and Brendan was
left with not much of a plan. Using the speedboat was dropped because of a
lack of time. Smuggling in a gun within a television for Colin was cancelled as
well. The boffin who had to fit the firearm into the TV in the factory he worked,
was on holiday in France for ten days. Brendan still had to arrange a car, guns
for outside and a safe house near the prison to change car and clothes. This
needed to be done in the next few days. To top it all off, Brendan received a
letter off his parents saying they would be visiting in two weeks time for three
days or more. As much as he hated the disgusting place where he had to
welcome two of the most decent people he knew, he would be pleased to see
them. But with that he now had a very serious problem. He really couldn't have
them visiting him at this time, but he couldn't say that on the phone. On these
days of all days they had to visit! Brendan needed to dream up something for it.

On the day before the escape Brendan's parents visited. They all
talked about the family and how everyone was. It was lovely to see them, and
they said they would visit again the next day. While every word was taped, he
had to make clear to them that the visit couldn't take place.
'I'm sorry, but tomorrow a friend will be visiting me' he lied out of sheer
necessity. It was moments like these in prison that really pissed him off. He truly

hated lying to his parents. He'd done it already too many times in his life. They were very understanding. Fortunately, they didn't ask difficult questions. Brendan felt troubled and relieved at the same time. Now he could fully concentrate on the escape.

## Chapter Fifteen: Now Or Never

The morning of the escape attempt was like every other morning. It was quiet on the unit. The plan was to strike on the way to the visiting room. They would capture the accompanying screws in the stairwell, on the way to the visiting room. Brendan had got hold of a knife from the screw's kitchen and had already checked that the metallic joint of the knife wouldn't trigger the detector.

Brendan was going to go with Mohammed. There were two other prisoners on the unit: the Turk Serhat O., who had just come a few weeks before to wait for his extradition to Germany, and a Dutch fellow called Martin C. They knew nothing about the breakout till the last minute. Mohammed had been told to wear a set of clothes under his tracksuit. Brendan did the same.

The Turk and the Dutchman were asked to go to the visit. They were given the opportinuty to join in the escape. 'No questions. It's now or never' Brendan emphasised. 'Will you come along?'

Both didn't need time to think and said 'Yes!'

It was hardly surprising. The unit life was zombie like and repetitive.

**'Mr. H. de Jong of the Coornhert Liga (a Dutch association for reform of criminal law) thinks that the current regime has changed the EBI-cell into a 'tomb'. 'Last year dangerous dynamics have arisen', De Jong says. 'Once there is a spectacular escape, the press screams blue murder and the regime is tightened. In reaction on this more hostages are taken and further restrictions are followed. It is panic policy. A stronger hardening of detention is completely useless. In De Schie prisoners two times had a gun at their disposal. Does it help then to reduce their airing or their telephone time? If they want to communicate with people outside the prison, they will do it if necessary through the heating pipe. It seems more sensible to me to create a situation in which they are not thinking about an escape all day'.**
*Source: NRC Handelsblad, Wednesday 7th April 1993*

Brendan was standing in the corridor of the unit looking down at the office, which was full of screws. They were talking to each other or watching the TV monitors. He didn't know who would be their escort, it could consist of three or four of them. Mohammed was walking up and down the unit, visibly tense. So was Brendan, he could feel the adrenalin pumping through his veins. He was hoping and praying that the doors would open. Within half an hour they would either be free or in deep trouble.

Brendan was surprised to see the bent screw walk in. He entered the office, talked to the screws, came out onto the unit and went to the workshop. As he walked by he said in a low voice 'The special squad has arrived to bring another prisoner. They're in the building now'. Brendan said nothing but smiled. With this squad around an attempt made no sense. He had to play for time till the moment they left. On his way out Brendan asked the screw what time it was and slipped in: 'When they leave, walk into the unit office. Make an excuse'. 'Okay, I will' he said. He was worth every penny.

Over the tannoy the call went out for the visiting hour. Brendan strolled up to Mohammed. 'We need more time' he whispered. 'Go to the toilet and stay there till I call you'. Silently he closed the door of the toilet behind him.

The door of the unit was being unlocked. Two screws were ready to escort the four men to the visiting unit. 'Mohammed is still in the toilet' Brendan said. A moment later he saw the bent screw come in the office and called to Mohammed: 'What's keeping you?' He understood the message and came out.

They left the unit through three sets of doors and approached a door with a security camera above it. One of the screws pushed the button to report in at the central doorkeeper, who looked on the monitor and opened the remote-controlled door. They entered the corridor and walked down towards the metal detector. As planned, the device didn't react on the knife Brendan had concealed. Only when the screws passed through with their keys, did the metal detector go off.

At the end of the corridor they went to the right towards another door with a camera and push button. The central doorkeeper cleared the way to the lift hall. Down they went in the elevator, got out and walked to the door across from it. This was the door to the circulation hall. All units led into this hall. This door was also opened from a distance by the central gatekeeper.

Both ends of the corridor had offices where the screws watched from. There were no blind spots. The procession of prisoners and screws turned left and just on the right was a door. Two screws behind a desk stood up. After saying a couple of things to each other they opened the door with a key, letting the men into the stairwell before locking it again. This was the moment to strike.

As they started to go up the first flight of stairs, Brendan pulled the knife out and grabbed the first screw's hair back. Putting the knife to his throat, he said: 'I'll cut your fucking throat open if we don't get any doors open'. Serhat and Martin grabbed the two other screws and bent their arms up their backs. They were in full command of the situation.

After waiting a few seconds they walked back down to the door they'd just come through. Brendan looked at Mohammed and the other two. They looked like they were determined. He nodded 'ready' and pressed the doorbell.

The same screw that had let them into the stairwell opened the door. Mohammed pulled him through the doorway by his shirt and twisted his arm up his back. His pal was told to get down on the floor. The screws were all pleading not to be hurt. It didn't surprise Brendan to hear them begging. One of them had been pig ignorant a week before over having a clean towel a day before laundry day. 'You just wait for a towel! You're nothing special in here!' he'd shouted at Brendan. At this moment he was pleading for his life. 'Shut up', Brendan said. 'You're nothing special in here!'

With the hostages they headed towards the slush doors. They were only seconds into the hall at the doors when the internal alarms went off. In a split second all the screws came out of the woodwork. Four of them ran directly towards the would-be escapees from up the corridor. When they saw their colleague with a knife at his throat they stopped. 'Get down! Lie yourself down on the ground and shut up' Brendan shouted. They knew they didn't have a choice and obeyed.

More screws were running from all over the prison. As Brendan arrived at the slush doors and pressed the bell there were about fifteen to twenty screws behind. After the first doors closed behind them, they waited a few tense seconds for the second doors to be opened. For a moment they actually were captured between the slush doors. The seconds seemed to last hours. To great relief they eventually heard a click. The second doors were open.

All seven went through, down a hallway into a reception area for visits, where a doorkeeper was sitting behind a glass partition. A second or two after he saw his colleague's face being pushed to the glass with a knife to his throat, the door was open. Finally, they were out in the front car park.

The car that was supposed to be waiting with our guns wasn't there. Brendan looked at Mohammed and said: 'What the fuck is going on?! Where's the car?'

'I don't know!' he answered. 'Let's just run'.

'Where is that car?!' he repeated.

'I swear I don't know' he called back.

The three screws they'd taken hostage were lying on the car park floor with their hands tied behind their backs. One of them still had the knife to his neck. Brendan asked him what kind of car he drove. 'A white Opel Kadett' he answered. 'I parked it in front of us'. Taking the keys Brendan threw them to Mohammed, who ran to the car. Looking over at the visitor entrance he could see that the whole glass windows were full of screw faces, staring out. None of them came outside, but the whole entrance was full of them.

Mohammed was having problems firing up the car. After several attempts the old diesel engine started. Mohammed pulled up, but after a few yards the old banger had stopped again. While the Turk and the Dutchman jumped onto the backseat of the car, Mohammed managed to restart the car again. He raced towards Brendan and stopped right in front with squeeling tyres. Brendan released the screws and jumped into the car, next to Moham-med, telling Martin to turn on the walkie-talkie they'd borrowed from a screw. They were then able to listen to the talk between the prison and the police. They sounded frantic.

'What clothes is Quinn wearing?'

'A black tracksuit'.

'What kind of car are they driving? Are they armed?'

Brendan took off his tracksuit, revealing the clothes he had on underneath.

He was wearing a shirt, tie and jeans now.
'And this Moroccan? What is he wearing?', it went on over the walkie-talkie.
'He's completely in white clothes'.
Behind the wheel Mohammed started to take off his white suit. Brendan couldn't believe his eyes. Underneath this suit he wore white clothes as well! There was no time to discuss it, but it was clear that this guy was totally nuts. They had to get out of the car they were in. The walkie talkie crackled with questions. Which way did they go? How many people? and so on.

Brendan knew that he had to get rid of Mohammed when he stopped at a red light. 'Mo, what the hell are you doing?' he asked.
'I don't want to attract attention by breaking the red light', he said.
Lost for words, Brendan explained quietly 'Look, Mohammed, every cop in the area is looking for this car and us by now. Fuck the lights and anything else that gets in our way! Drive!' From that moment Mohammed broke every set of red lights.

There was a safe house in Overschie, a suburb a couple of miles away. As they got close, Brendan told Mohammed to pull into a side street. They stopped, got out and Brendan handed the keys to Martin and the Turk, shaking hands with them and wishing them luck. The Turkish guy wouldn't let his hand go while saying things in Turkish. Brendan didn't understand nor had he time to listen, but he could understand that he was very grateful.

Mohammed and Brendan walked off a couple of hundred yards apart. They could hear police sirens going off all around. Reaching the house, they went in to change and went straight out to a second car that was waiting there for them. Behind the wheel was a girl, who drove them out of this suburb, onto the motorway. Brendan sat up front, next to her with Mohammed lying down in the back with a blanket over him. As they drove out of Rotterdam they could see several police check points being set up.

**'Four extremely armed and dangerous criminals have escaped from the special secured unit of the Rotterdam prison De Schie yesterday. The umpteenth getaway this year has caused even more indignation because the brain behind the escape, the 29 years old Irish professional criminal Brendan Q., was only last Monday convicted to ten years imprisonment. The escape took place after a taking of hostages. Three guards literally had a knife put to their throat.**
**The Amsterdam court sentenced the unscrupulous Brendan Q. last Monday due to his part in the sensational armed robbery and hostage taking of the work force of the C1000-supermarket, last spring in Amsterdam. The State Secretary of Justice Mr. Kosto will take extra security measures at prisons. 'If necessary, we must reduce the rights of prisoners to a safe minimum, if this enables us to keep the people inside'.**
**The Irishman Brendan also escaped on the 13th of January from a jail for**

long-term prisoners in Sittard. In England Brendan Q. partly evaded an imprisonment of four years by escaping there as well.

The hunt of the police for the four fugitives is focussed on Amsterdam, because two of the criminals – the Irishman Brendan Q. and the Dutchman M.C. – have good contacts in the capital city.

During the massive search operation, directly after the escape, both decks of the Van Brienenoord bridge were opened for twenty minutes. By artificially creating a traffic-jam on the highway, the police intended to search for the car of the four fugitives. This however had no result.

In De Schie yesterday there were 248 prisoners. The special secured unit of the prison counts eight cells for high risk detainees. Since yesterday afternoon half of these cells are empty...

*Source: De Telegraaf, Friday 4th September 1992.*

## Chapter Sixteen: The Chase

Behind them Brendan could see the cars closest to them hitting a red light. He took a deep breath and exhaled vigorously. The skyline of Rotterdam disappeared behind the horizon. For the first time that day he started to relax and asked the girl to pull in at a motorway garage. He went in and bought a newspaper and cigarettes. He made a couple of phone calls to friends and looked around. Everyone was busy going in and out, oblivious to anything around them. He couldn't help thinking that he'd normally be locked up in a poxy cell if he was in that dreary horrible unit in De Schie right now. It was good to be out.

'**The management of De Schie was braced for some time that an escape could occur, or high mounting conflicts could arise inside the prison walls. For that reason, a change of personnel was carried out last month. Inexperienced jailors inside the special secured unit changed places with more experienced colleagues. Reason for this measure was the plan to considerably sharpen the EBI-regime by the 1st of September.**
**The management feared that Brendan Q. would react to this. One of the measures to be taken would affect the Irishman personally. Some cells, including his, would get new windows, which could not be opened.**'
*Source: De Telegraaf, Tuesday 8th September 1992.*

'**Directly after the escape of the extremely dangerous four, last Thursday, the other four EBI-prisoners of De Schie were submitted to a heavier re-gime. 'We are locked in our cell for twenty hours a day now', one of them complains. The latest escape paves the way to an even heavier approach. In the temporary empty EBI-cells of B.Q, M.M, S.O. and M.C, new windows are being fitted.**'
*Source: De Telegraaf, Saturday 12th September 1992*

Brendan went back to the car and they left, heading to a flat in Groningen. He didn't have the faintest notion where it was. He just knew once they were in a safe house, he could arrange everything by phone. Eventually they pulled in at a block of flats. Their's was on the top floor. It was quite a big flat and modern too. Brendan asked the girl to phone his friend up as soon as she got back to Amsterdam. She was then to bring him to the flat. She said it would take a few hours. 'No problem. Just make sure you leave the getaway car in Amsterdam and come back with my friend's car'. He gave her a kiss and said: 'Thanks. I owe you'.

While Mohammed started to cook some chicken and pasta, Brendan took a long shower. Back in the living room he plumped down into a sofa. 'What do you think? Will the 'scream' over the escape be on the news and in the papers?' he asked. Mohammed shrugged. 'Perhaps. Anyway, they won't find us easily. The Dutch are very reserved in putting names or pictures in the newspapers or on TV. They will just write some stuff in the paper, but nothing more than our descriptions.' This made Brendan feel easier. He'd made his mind up while they were driving that he wasn't going to do anything in Holland. He would get money off a couple of friends and use that to leave with. He didn't want to do any more robberies in Holland. It had become too hot.

**'The escape of four dangerous, professional criminals from the special secured part of the Rotterdam prison, is a straight attempt on the constitutional state.'**
*Source: editorial comment De Telegraaf, Saturday 5th September 1992.*

Deep in thought Brendan thumbed through the post on the table. He noticed a name on it that Mohammed had something to do with. It was the same name of someone that had visited him in De Schie. He looked at it again to make sure. 'Mohammed!', he said, 'What's this?!', showing him the letter. 'Well, that's nothing serious. It's the sister of a friend of mine who visited me once. Nothing to worry about.'
'Right. That's clear! Let's get out of here!'. Brendan jumped up, grabbed his coat and said to Mohammed: 'What do you think you're doing? This is much too risky! They might decide to do a few raids in the morning. That would include anyone connected with prison visits living in Holland!'
'Oh well, we can stay another night, can't we?', said Mohammed with a poker face, while he shuffled back to his pots and pans.
'No way! Let's go!' Brendan said. Ten minutes later they were walking down the street and Brendan called another friend, who gave him details for another safe address, somewhere in Groningen.
When they arrived, Brendan pressed the doorbell of the safe house. A woman opened the door. 'Come in quickly' she said. It was quite early that evening when she said that she was going to bed already. 'If you wake up tomorrow, I won't be there. My shift is starting very early in the morning'. When Brendan asked her what kind of work she did, her answer almost knocked him out. 'I'm working at the prison. I'm a jailor'.
The surprises that day didn't seem to end. Brendan didn't feel at all comfortable, but his contacts were very reliable, so they spent the night in her flat.
The next morning, after she'd gone to work at the prison, they left. It felt a little strange spending his first night of freedom in a screw's flat!
In the afternoon Mohammed phoned the girl who'd driven them out of Rotterdam. She picked up Brendan's friend in Amsterdam, but back in Groningen they had found a deserted flat. She said that the friend had left a telephone number, a couple of hand guns and some money for them. He rang the number given and arranged a meeting for the next day.

Meanwhile Brendan and Mohammed were going to a flat owned by a Somalian plumber. His girlfriend opened the door and didn't know who they were but it was perfect to stay in for a couple of days or so.

Two days after the escape Mohammed showed Brendan De Telegraaf. He couldn't believe his eyes. Under the headline 'Justice releases picture of four jailbreakers' both their photos were published. Mohammed translated the article:

**'The Ministry of Justice decided yesterday to release pictures of the four extremely dangerous criminals who escaped from the Rotterdam prison De Schie last Thursday during a spectacular incident. The reason is to simplify the tracing of the armed and dangerous four.**
**According to a spokesman of the Justice Department the decision to release the photos is made because 'the privacy of these people doesn't balance the social danger they provide'.**
**The police emphasise that the four are very dangerous and armed and ask for the help of the public. To give information about the present where-abouts of the four, the Rotterdam police have opened a telephone number: 010-xxxxxxx.'**
*Source: De Telegraaf, Saturday 5th September 1992*

Brendan was surprised to learn of the fuss their escape had apparently caused and was astonished by the photos on the front page. The article in the paper really hotted things up for them moving from A to B. He knew he had to leave Holland as soon as he could.

Five days had passed by since the escape, when De Telegraaf published an article about Brendan's background. They had found out that his parents were in Holland and that they had visited him in the week before he'd broke out. From this, they concluded that his parents were involved in the escape. Worse than that though, they were accused of being the brains behind an IRA operation!

**'The IRA – the Irish Republican Army – is most likely involved in the escape of four heavy criminals from the Rotterdam prison De Schie last week. An investigation by this newspaper shows that the parents of Brendan Q. – who are fervent supporters of the IRA – spent the weeks in advance of the escape in Rotterdam. The parents of Q. have disappeared since last Wednesday.'**
*Source: De Telegraaf, Tuesday 8th September 1992.*

'What a lot of shit!' Brendan thought to himself. It was complete nonsense. It was not the first time this kind of crap had been written about his background. One paper wrote that he was sentenced to four years in London for a murder, the other paper reported that he had to do sixteen years for armed robberies. The Justice Department in Holland provided the Dutch media with false information. They stated as fact that Brendan had committed a murder, even though he'd never been prosecuted for a crime like that. Even in the official report about the escape from De Geerhorst it was written that he had killed someone. It wasn't that surprising, because the authorities couldn't even spell his name. They even managed to give him another nationality.

**'The Centrale Recherche Informatiedienst (the central criminal investigation and information service, CRI) received information that Q. was convicted due to armed robberies and had to do sixteen years.'**
*Source: ANP, Monday 14th October 1991.*

**'According to the Dutch police Quinn is wanted for an armed and fatal robbery.'**
*Source: The Evening Herald, Wednesday 15th January 1992.*

**'The 28 years old man had escaped in 1988 from prison, where he was being held following different robberies.'**
*Source: De Telegraaf, Tuesday 4th June 1991.*

**'The Irishman B.Q. is suspected of violence and has to be in prison for sixteen years in the United Kingdom for murder, but he has disappeared without a trace.'**
*Source: Algemeen Dagblad, Thursday 16th January 1992.*

**'On Thursday 30th August 1991 the detainee Brendan QUIN, born on 9th May 1963, with no permanent home or address in this country and of English nationality, has been locked in into the house of detention in Sittard. (...) Detainee Quin was placed in the system of the Extra Beveiligde Inrichting (special secured unit) because he escaped from a prison in England, where he was serving a lengthy imprisonment because of a murder he committed. The man is reputed to be aggressive, dangerous and strong.'**
*Source: Justice, file nr. 6030-42-1992, The escape of Londoño and Quin on 14th January 1992.*

Brendan knew these ridiculous rumours about their connection with the IRA made his parents feel very nervous. They stayed in Holland, but the Dutch police had set up surveillance on them and openly followed them round the country. His father said he had more protection than the prime minister of Holland with all those policemen following them.

The flat Brendan was staying in with Mohammed was a small studio flat in Veenwouden, a small village in the northern province of Friesland. When you opened the front door, you could see the whole flat, which was just one room. It was suitable for now and a lot better than a cell in some poxy jail, especially a security unit, where you were locked in a small cell up to 23 hours a day.

Brendan's friends arrived that evening and came up to the flat. He asked them to arrange two passports - one for Mohammed and one for him - money and a safe route out of Holland. They said they would fix it all. 'We have never seen such a big fuss over an escape before' one of them said. 'You were on the national television news, with photos and everything'. The guys left a short time after. They arranged to come back the next night and tell them when they'd be leaving.

The next day Brendan and Mohammed stayed in the flat and just relaxed. That evening the friends came back. They'd arranged everything. Within a few days Brendan could leave by ship from Rotterdam. The passports would be ready by then. They left some money and went out.

It was around 10 p.m. when they came back again. 'You can take the ferry tomorrow morning. It will leave at 8 a.m.' they said. They suggested Brendan could go with them right away and drive to a safe house near Rotterdam, but he didn't like that idea. Instead he decided to stay in the flat another night, get picked up in the morning and go straight to the ship from here. He arranged for a bike to collect him ealry next morning and head for Rotterdam.

Mohammed didn't want to leave Holland. 'You won't get any distance in Holland while you're under the spotlight like this' Brendan warned him. But Mohammed couldn't be convinced. He seemed to just want to leave. It was getting on for midnight when Brendan told him: 'If you want to go, just go, but you should have left earlier.' But off they went. Brendan watched TV for a while and went to bed. He couldn't sleep right away, he was thinking about leaving the next morning. It was only a few hours away. He didn't know where Mohammed had gone. He'd only got a number to ring for his passport and a little money for travelling. Eventually Brendan fell asleep.

First came an enormous explosion, followed by a shrieking whistle in his ears and a blinding white light through his eyelids. While Brendan was floating between dream and reality, he tried to remember where he was. A second later a hood was put over his head, guns held to his head and his hands were cuffed behind his back. Only then did it dawn on him that the front door had been blown out and a disorientation bomb thrown into the house. A special squad had captured him.

Only one thought kept going through his mind: Which dirty rat told them where to find me?' There's no way they knew it from police work. They had to have been told.

They pushed his head down to the floor. After a while they lifted it again, raising the hood a bit. In a glimpse he saw a map with a torch shining on it. A voice said: 'Where are the others?' Brendan didn't answer him. He just wanted to know how they knew he was there. Another voice said through the hood: 'Nice friends you have! Calling the police to betray you!' A phone call to the police? That in itself didn't give Brendan any answers.

**'The Irishman who escaped in January as well didn't offer resistance against his arrest by the inter-regional special squad. According to the leader of the investigation to the four escaped prisoners - the Rotterdam public prosecutor Mr. W. Wabeke - the man was alone in the house and unarmed. Justice is satisfied that they managed to arrest the Irishman as the first one of the four. 'His escape caused the most anxiety', Wabeke said. According to eyewitnesses the special squad first entered the wrong house with an infernal noise around 5:00 p.m.'**
*Source: Algemeen Dagblad, Thursday 10th September 1992.*

Brendan was taken down to a car and driven to a police station. The cops who arrested him turned out to be members of the special squad of the state police in Leeuwarden. They put him in a small cell with no window. He couldn't believe this had happened, despite all the caution and work in the six days since the escape. He was as pissed off as a person could be.
Some fucking rat had grassed.

He sat down and thought about this for the next few hours before the cell door opened. He was being moved to Veenhuizen. On 22nd September, less than three weeks after their escape, Mohammed was caught. In the heat of the night he was arrested in his bed in Rotterdam. The arrest of Martin was one day later in Amsterdam. The Turk was never heard from again.

In November 1992 Brendan was on the move again. First they moved him to Veenhuizen for one night. Early the next morning though he was up and away again. It seemed they just didn't know what to do with him. Brendan hoped he would end up in Hoogeveen. He knew he wouldn't make the same mistake again and would make sure to leave the country the same day of any escape.

Eventually they didn't bring him to any of the four EBI's, but to one of the prison towers of the Bijlmerbajes in Amsterdam. Brendan had already stayed in the Bijlmerbajes once after the robberies on Albert Heijn and the hotel and the tram-hijacking. Now, however he was there with a punishment regime with tight limitations. It turned out that the EBI's had been shut down, due to the fact they had largely failed to tackle the problem they had been set up for. Until Justice had found a definitive alternative for the EBI's, prisoners of the heavy calibre were transported to 'control-problematic units'.

The Bijlmerbajes tower accommodated one of the three prisons with so called national isolation facilities. The two other prisons of this type were in

Maastricht and Veenhuizen. After a month in Amsterdam Brendan was transferred to Maastricht, in the very south of the Netherlands. He didn't know this prison at all. Once again, he would need to find and map the weak spots in the security.

## Chapter Seventeen: Getting Out Of Maastricht

The so-called close confinement wing of the bricked prison tower Over-maze in Maastricht is situated on the top floor. It's called the K-wing, an isolation unit where prisoners end up when they have proved to be 'uncontrollable' in a regular prison. In such circumstances a so-called measure of confinement is issued, which has to be executed in Maastricht. Mostly a prisoner is held there two to four weeks in this punishment wing.

The philosophy is that the prisoner has to earn everything back again. For example, after a few days good behaviour you get a plastic spoon, then a knife and eventually a fork. After a week of good behaviour your night light is switched off. And if you're really good, you can have a television and make phone calls. This didn't apply to Brendan. For seven months he wasn't allowed to send or receive letters. The light at night had been on for months. No nothing. At most, he should have been held there for one month like every other prisoner.

The staff there were a bunch of real arseholes, barring two. Brendan often heard the screws beating up other prisoners. This always pissed him off. He would just love to have been able to walk out and even the odds, when a guy next door was getting beaten by them. This one day the thuds could be heard plainly through the wall of his cell, as they kicked and punched whoever the unfortunate fellow was. Brendan got up and started kicking the door. A screw lifted the spy flap and said: 'Stop that immediately!'
'Bollocks! You stop hitting him next door'. He let the flap down. Brendan started kicking the door again. From the noises he could hear from behind the door and the groans it was clear that the fellow was badly hurt. He was being carried off to the strip cell.

A few minutes later Brendan's cell door was opened. It was the usual little gang of screws. He'd been put on a rule where six screws would unlock the door together. There was one big fat screw, saying in his best English: 'If you bang your door or say anything, you will be next!' Brendan walked over to him at the door. 'Try me, you fat fuck! They'll be bringing you and me to the hospital together. I'll bite chunks out of your throat!'
Staring for a few seconds, the screw replied: 'You're an animal' and slammed the door.

To go for air, Brendan had to go over to the small shower which was two steps from his cell door, directly opposite. There he would take off his overalls and shorts, give them to a screw to search and then receive new ones. He would then have to put one leg on the shower bench. The screws would use a mirror, attached to a stick and look up his arse, what they were checking for Brendan never knew. Of course, this procedure didn't have anything to do with safety rules. It was just their way of getting revenge.

Brendan always went for air. Despite them only daring to take him out for just thirty minutes to a cell on the roof. This particular morning he was going up in the lift to the roof. The screws were all staring at him. One of them, a bodybuilder, asked Brendan why he was looking at him. In an equally aggressive tone he answered: 'It's because you completely disgust me, you dog!' Brendan noticed that the screw didn't know how to react in this situation. In the end he decided to ask for back up. When the lift doors opened, there were five to seven screws, their batons ready, about to rush the lift. It looked like they were out for blood. That was a different story. He would make sure if that was what they wanted, if they were going to be personal, the situation would change irrevocable. Brendan could read on their faces they thought they would get away with it, but what a mistake they would be making. He would go to any length to retaliate inside and especially outside the jail.

From that moment the tension was permanent. Every time Brendan's door was opened you could cut the air. They hated each other. The days turned into weeks, still there was just bare hatred on that wing. Eventually he found out why the bodybuilder was such an imbecile. His brother had worked in Sittard EBI when Brendan escaped there with Ruben Londoño. Apparently, he was upset because his brother had been there at the time.

One tea time on the K-wing a big screw was being real chatty. People knew him as a former Dutch judo champion. He challenged Brendan to try and get out of a neck hold. Brendan said: 'If you try one, I will'. As he reached out for the bread, the screw grabbed him, hoilding him in the Lord Nelson hold: from behind he stuck his arms under Brendan's armpits and folded his hands together around his neck. By stretching his neck and upper arms, Brendan pulled off his hands, grabbed his arm and half hunched at the same time pulled him over his head in high throw. He landed on his back. All the screws were just looking at their colleague on the floor, holding his back. Brendan just said: 'Bang my door up' and walked into the cell. The judo man had to stay off for a few days.

During a phonecall to friends Brendan made it clear he wasn't happy with things there. Two days later a couple of friends, husband and wife, came over to visit but they were refused entry. They had the police called on them but they wouldn't leave until they knew Brendan was alright. A visit was arranged for the following week, when the wife would come. When she arrived for the rescheduled visit, as she entered, she said something about the doors in Irish. The four screws, who were present, demanded she speak English. They had notepads out to write down every single word spoken, even though the entire meeting was taped on video and audio and a glass partition separated them from Brendan.

On the visit Brendan asked her to give a friend a car he had in her garage and a few thousand guilders he'd had left there. He told her to tell the friend that the car needed a new water pump. That's why he'd parked it up. The rest of the visit he just listened to her talking about life outside. When they were finished six screws took Brendan to the strip cell, which is a cell with nothing at all in it. In there you only wear your underwear. Brendan stayed in this cell for six weeks, with his visiting rights suspended, because they assumed that during the visit they'd been speaking in code. Brendan wouldn't answer anything about what was said, when questioned.

After the six weeks had passed he got his cell back again and it was back to the mind-numbing routine with the screws. There was no love lost and Brendan could barely contain the hate he had for them. He didn't see what gave them the right to beat prisoners unconscious in there.

It was early one evening when he heard someone at the door. Usually his door only opened at air and meal times. This was neither. The head screw opened up and said: 'Brendan, do you mind if we come in and talk to you?' 'No, come in. Say what you have to say.' Brendan went to the back of the cell by the window. All these screws came in, the cell was full of them.

'Brendan', the head screw said, 'usually no one is kept here as long as you have been kept here. Anyone who stays a month in here, changes. You have been here almost a year and you haven't changed. You've got colder towards us. We know that you would use anyone of us as a hostage to get out. All we're saying is if you do take a hostage, none of us will try to stop you. Just don't hurt the hostage. And one other thing: we want to tell you it's not been said to another prisoner before, but we all respect you. We want to know if you respect us too.'

'Respect is something I don't give lightly' he answered. 'I certainly wouldn't even think of respect for your people. I would say you're getting respect confused with toleration.' Brendan didn't say anything about potential hostages, because it really didn't matter what they thought if he made a move. They had no choice anyway. 'That was all?' he asked. They left.

Watching them go he wondered what had happened outside to get to this situation. It sounded like they were trying to say the usual bollocks the screws came out with: 'I'm just doing my job'. Well, so were the soldiers who hammered the nails into the hands of Jesus. Fuck them! They had gone too far already. They'd killed every contact with his family, they were aggressive and this mirror they used to look at his arse had nothing to do with guarding a prisoner. The way they treated him was completely over the top.

One night, sitting in his cell on the K-wing, about 10 p.m., Brendan's door suddenly opened. Two real halfwits were standing there with guns. 'Show me your hands!' one of them shouted. Brendan thought something was wrong, but it was just another surprise search, with dogs and guns. Fucking people! Intimidations, screws with guns and dogs in his cell. If Brendan had done that to someone in their house, he'd have got fifteen to twenty years for it!

It was the same kind of behaviour of the BOT-team that used to bring him to his court appearances. They didn't have to put the heavy black canvas bag on his head. They could have used the light one. When you have been in a little cell for months or years and then being cuffed, hooded and driven in a high-powered car one morning, the motion will make you feel sick as a dog.

To get fresh air on the way to the court, Brendan would use a simple trick. The day before the ride he would chew very slowly a couple of raw garlic cloves. The next day, when they were driving, he'd take extra long breaths and breathe out slowly. After a few minutes they always opened the windows on each side of him. Under the hood he would just smile to himself.

Brendan never considered escaping while on escort or in court. There was too much security. They had marksmen on the roofs by the court and police in the court, armed with automatics. No, he would go from prison. It was quieter that way.

Soon Brendan was ready to break out of the K-wing. In his cell the ceiling could be pushed up. He'd hidden six sheets up there, putting one sheet in the laundry bag instead of two. But after a few weeks they started to count all the sheets each week. The plan was to make a rope and smash out the window one night. He was fourteen floors up, but Brendan was fit enough to climb down using the sheets. But he hadn't got enough. He made another plan, which got more solid by the day. All he needed to do was arrange a car and driver at the front of the jail. It had to happen during breakfast, dinner or tea time, when he was out of his cell. Problem was however that Brendan just had no solid way of communicating. He could get out of Maastricht, but he needed to be driven away. He didn't have a clue where he was.

Brendan had made a weapon from the steel clip in the little wardrobe, taking it off and scraping it to razor sharpness. This would do fine to take one of the screws with. He used to look at them at the door. They looked like those deer that used to go for a drink and watched for the crocodiles. One day he'd roared BOO! while they were at the door. They jumped quickly back. Brendan had closed the door with his foot and walked in with his tea, laughing so much he had tears in his eyes.

He was concentrating on getting out so much that some other things escaped his notice. When they came for him early one morning and the cell was filled with screws, members of the special squad and dogs, all he thought was they were on the wind up again. He was told to grab his things together. Had he missed something? Did he have to be in court today? No, he would have known for sure. Instead, he was on the move again.

The ride took more time than usual. They escorted him from the deepest south of the Netherlands up to the north-east, to punishment jail De Rode Pannen (The Red Tiles) in Veenhuizen. Brendan didn't mind it there. The cells were much bigger and had plenty of air. The usual conditions were still in place though: isolation, no contact. It was inhumane.

He was glad to be out of Maastricht. Escaping from there would have been too awkward without outside help.

One morning Brendan got a letter from his brother, who was in another Dutch jail. He mentioned that if he was ever in Veenhuizen Brendan had to look up the social worker or psychologist. He'd never before asked to speak to anybody. Quite the contrary, he'd always told them to fuck off. A few days later though, his curiosity got the better of him and he asked to see this man. None of the screws could believe it, nor could Brendan! He only wanted to see if Tony had given him a message without the fellow knowing he's saying it. It turned out that there was nothing like that. The man however seemed genuinely concerned at his treatment. He was one of the only genuine ones Brendan met in prison life. He asked to see him again but Brendan just sent him his regards. To tell the truth, he felt embarrassed by it. All those jail house shrinks and psychologists are pro system. Anyway, they can only help the vulnerable.

In Maastricht and Veenhuizen Brendan overheard bits of talk in Dutch both on TV and radio about the creation of a super-EBI: an ultramodern jail for the heaviest criminals of the nation. No one would be able to escape from there. The Netherlands was at the beginning of a new detention era, it was said. All special secured units had to be changed for one hundred percent 'waterproof' bunkers.

**'All maximum-security prisoners will temporary be accommodated in penitentiary Nieuw Vosseveld in Vught during the summer. The main building in the centre of Nieuw Vosseveld will be prepared for it.'**
*Source: De Telegraaf, Saturday 24th April 1993.*

Naturally, it made Brendan feel uneasy. The security would have no end. He would hate to be in a prison he knew he couldn't get out of. The bad thing going against him in Holland was he'd already showed his hand with the escapes from London, Sittard and Rotterdam. He knew there'd been a lot of stuff in the newspapers about his escapes, but he had no idea how much coverage or detail there had been. He hadn't spoken to hardly anyone in over a year. Practically no contact with the outside world. It seemed they were prepared to spend millions and millions on anything that would prevent escapes.

## Chapter Eighteen: Incomunicado

This move wasn't any different to the way the BOT usually moved him. They just all seemed extra serious. Brendan didn't know where he was going this time. Maybe back to Maastricht or one of the units again. He'd had been totally isolated from the outside world for almost a year now and hadn't been allowed to use the phone, write or read any letters. The screws called him an incommunicado.

He could tell they were close to the place when the police stopped talking and started making hand signals. He could sense the body movement. Brendan was right. A couple of minutes later they had arrived at the Amster- dam prison Bijlmerbajes, which was the only one of its kind. The tower blocks were fourteen stories high, it was the highest Brendan had ever seen. His cell would be in the notorious tower called Demersluis, on the top floor isolation unit. They'd even moved all the other prisoners off before he arrived.

It was just a cell with nothing in it besides a mattress. They had made him face the wall of the cell, taken the handcuffs off and then the hood. From behind him he heard the cell door shut and the outside bolts go on. The window, if you could call it that, was blackened, so it was hard to see out.

It was afternoon. Brendan laid on the mattress and thought through the situation in his mind. The extra prison security that he'd been under since his arrest after the De Schie breakout was not relaxing. There was always half a dozen of them together when the door was being opened.

Here the routine was the same as the past year, except for some extra, bizarre rules. He had half an hour exercise a day, at all different times of the day or night. Every time he had to take the overalls off. No underwear was permitted, no footwear either, except prison slippers. When it was time to go for his half hour air, he first had to remove the overalls and stand naked with hands against the far wall, fingers spread and legs apart. The head screw would look through the hatch in the door, then he would say 'turn around and walk slowly to the door'. When he got to the door, he would have to walk across the hall into the wash room. Still naked. If he was lucky, he could go into the shower for five minutes. Mostly though, they only let Brendan have a sink wash and brush his teeth. After drying off he then had to put on different overalls, which were never the right size. Only then could he go next door to take the air.

The air cell was a kind of prison cell. The only different was this cell simply had a cast-iron grid on the roof instead of a ceiling. That was the exercise yard!

They never left Brendan alone for one second. Undressing, showering, drying off and airing, they always had him in sight.

The screws on this unit were members of the LBB (Landelijke Bijzon- dere Bijstandsverlening), the national special assistance unit. The LBB are the riot police of the Dutch prison system. They were specially trained to handle people like Brendan. Whenever they came to let him out for air, they would have long batons, shields, helmets and body protection. Five of them would be dressed like this. The team leader was just in uniform.

He didn't like walking naked and taking a shower in front of these people. Sometimes female screws were also there with batons, shields and helmets. They would always make a semi circle around him and close in behind, when he went into the cell, shower room or exercise cell. They had no reason to be so over the top. Brendan hadn't had visits or phone calls, letters, nothing for nearly a year. In effect nobody even knew he was there!

**'The circumstances under which prisoners are being kept in the special secured unit of De Schie in Rotterdam and the unit for highly problematic prisoners in Demersluis in Amsterdam are quite poor. The cells themselves are of good quality, but especially in the maximum secured unit 4A of Demersluis the regime is far too restrictive and the relations between employees and detainees very bad. This has to change very quickly, says the Council of Europe in Strasbourg in an investigative report about the prison system in the Netherlands, which was presented today.'**
*Source: NRC Handelsblad, Thursday 15th July 1993.*

One morning Brendan told the head screw he had some complaints. The screw was listening through the hatch in the cell door. 'I don't like this way I have to go to to take air' Brendan said, 'especially with women present plus two big CCTV cameras at each end of the hallway. And the food is completely shit! I also want to write a letter and phone my family and lawyer'.
'I'll be back in a minute' he said and walked away. He came back a little later with the jail governor, Mr. J. Elbers (appendix 3), a fat, oldish ugly man who was very ignorant. He started to read a sheet of paper to Brendan in Dutch. He didn't understand a word of it. 'Say it in English', he said.
'This is a letter from the Justice-secretary of state in The Hague. It says you have to do your penalty in isolation and under this regime' he said. He wasn't allowed to cut his hair or shave. Nothing sharp was to be left in case he used it.

**'Partly based on an advice of the Penitentiary Selection Centre I have asked you to receive detainee B. Quinn and put him in pavilion IV, intended for detainees who cause a controllability risk in extreme extent. (...) It is my firm belief that isolation is strongly recommended, considering the personality of the person involved, and he is at the moment completely unfit to stay in limited community.**
**The person involved shows desperado-like behaviour, characterised by strong manipulative tendencies. He expresses his intention to escape repeatedly. Whenever he sees a chance, he doesn't hesitate to use force or violence. He is constantly focussed on possible weak spots in the**

security system. Besides that, he shows a pathological interest in materials which could be useful to him in an attempt to escape, especially materials that could be used as a tool by taking violent action to force employees to gratify his wishes.'
*Source: letter of Secretary of State A. Kosto (Ministry of Justice) to Demersluis Governor J.E.A. Elbers, Friday 20th November 1992.*

The only thing Brendan got out of this meeting at his door was the right to use a battery shaver, and that was even too late, because his beard was already started. He knew from this meeting that this ugly old man had serious intent to hold him like this.

The situation was hopeless. In addition, the Ministry of Justice was trying to take away Brendan's rights of getting released early, after two thirds of the punishment, which is usual in the Netherlands.

'The 30 year old Irishman B.Q. seems set to lose his early release. With that he is one of the first criminals who are the 'victims' of a sharpened policy against misbehaving detainees. The penitentiary chamber of the court of justice in Arnhem yesterday dealt with the requisitioning of the Procurator-General in Amsterdam to withdraw the early release.
(…) The case against Q. is one of the first this year since the Prosecution Counsel, as a consequence of the wish of the parliament and the minister of Justice Hirsch Ballin, is asking more frequently to cancel the early release.'
*Source: Het Parool, Tuesday 7th September 1993.*

Once again there was only one solution: escaping and leaving Holland. He had to get out of there at any cost. Without outside help, which he couldn't arrange unless he had visits or other contact, this would be very difficult to plan properly.

The relationship between Brendan and this LBB squad was deteriorating by the day. The food they brought each day was never even warm and above all just disgusting. Even a pig would walk away from it. He decided to completely ignore the screws, except if he had to be aired or fed. Brendan asked for a small piece of paper and a pencil. Tearing the paper in two, on one piece he wrote YES, on the other NO. He would simply show one of these if he was asked for dinner, exercise or tea. This way he wouldn't have to talk to these idiots any longer.

Brendan exercised for three to four hours a day in his cell, to remain in shape physically and mentally. He did a lot of stretching and yoga and observed a tight sports schedule, which he worked through since the moment they'd put him in the isolation unit in Maastricht. In the morning he would do 3000 sit ups and 1000 press ups. The 3000 sit ups took him one hour to do. He did the 1000 press ups in four sets of 250 each. But physically he didn't make any progress. He was losing weight from the shit food they tried to feed him in Demersluis. It became harder and harder not to weaken.

If he wasn't eating Brendan knew that he had to drink well so he drank eight small paper cup fulls in the morning and eight in the evening. Every single request for a cup of water was followed by the same procedure: He had to stand as far as possible from the door with his hands against the wall and legs and fingers spread. They would place the paper cup on the little hatch shelf and move back. Then he was allowed to turn around slowly, walk over to the shelf, take the water, drink it and return to the wall. Just to drink water this was happening sixteen times a day.

One day Brendan heard an infernal racket in the building. In one of the four cells of the isolation unit was a lot of banging, drilling and wailing going on. He could smell metal being heated. These activities went on for a couple of days. When the noise was over later that week, he was on his way back to his cell after an airing. At least, that was what he expected. On his return they opened the door of the cell in which they had been working. It had metal sheets screwed in and soldered against the cell walls. Without saying a word, they shoved Brendan into this cell with steel walls. From that moment he was kept in there. The penetrating smell of the burnt metal stayed in the iron isolation cell for a week.

At night time the LBB would go home and the normal screws would bring tea. One night his hatch opened and a black face said rudely: 'Tea or not?' Looking him in the eyes Brendan realised t was the same screw who had been rude to him before when he was held here, before going to the EBI of De Geer-horst in Sittard.

That time he had snatched the milk off Brendan very rudely, when all he did was pick it up off the trolley and pour a bit into his tea. Then he had slammed the door shut in his face. It had annoyed Brendan so much so that he put a can of fruit into two long socks and waited for his door to open. When it did, he'd walked out of the cell – which was strictly forbidden – and kicked over the tray with the tea and stuff on it. He'd wanted to give this wanker a wake-up call in the form of a few belts from the can of fruit and was quite disappointed when he wasn't there. The other screws were just standing still, scared of what he'd do. 'Where is that ignorant fucking pig?!' Brendan asked. 'He's gone home' they squeaked. Other screws had come running out the office and Brendan walked over near them to see if the black screw was there. He wasn't so he just walked into his cell and closed the door after telling them: 'Keep that arsehole away from me or I'll give him more brain damage than he already obviously has.'

Brendan knew more about this screw than he realised. After his escape from Sittard EBI he'd visited a bent screw and gotten all kind of information about his ignorant colleague. Brendan knew where he lived, where he went for a beer and more of this kind of information. He'd even visited his favourite pub one evening, hoping to see him. Brendan hated the wanker.

Seeing his face again brought up his anger again. He hadn't changed. Brendan could tell by his look he thought he'd forgotten him. 'Hey, you shit for brains! I visited your flat!' Brendan shouted and mentioned his address and door number. He was scared stiff. 'If I see your poxy face ever again at the door, I will personally make sure you will be visited!'

When Brendan told him his address, he realised not to push his luck, because he never saw him again. He did report Brendan to the governor, but that meant nothing to him. He couldn't care less about that rubbish, but was glad that he never saw his face again for the rest of the stay.

This oppressive routine in Demersluis went on and on. They were trying their best to get him down. One day the hatch opened for the dinner to be pushed through. Brendan got up off the floor and took it without a word. It looked disgusting. He guessed it was supposed to be spaghetti bolognese. It was in one solid piece and cold. Beside it on the plastic tray was yoghurt spilt into the desert part. Just as he was about to sit down, he heard a voice say 'Hey, hey'. Brendan looked over to see a screw with his helmet on and visor down, who said: 'I'm saying this to let you know: don't eat the food here. They are doing sick things to it'. He shut the hatch and was gone.

Brendan looked at the food, picked it up and slammed it against the hatch. 'Dirty bastards!' From that moment on, he hardly ate anything except bread and cheese.

**'AMSTERDAM – With the long-lasting isolation of the 30 years old Irish detainee B.Q. the Amsterdam house of detention Demersluis has 'exceeded all bounds of reasonableness and fairness'. That is the judgement of the appeal committee from the Supervisory Commission after a complaint of B.Q. against the management of Demersluis. The lawyer of the detainee, Mr. N.C.J. Meijering, will report maltreatment by the manager. B.Q. is transferred by now to the temporary special secured institution (TEBI) in Vught, where in the future all maximum secured prisoners will be concentrated. Q. is known in the prison system as an 'escape artist'. Since his arrival on August 23 in Demersluis B.Q. stays in an isolation cell. He is being watched there with cameras and five members of the national special assistance unit LBB. He is not allowed to have contact with the outside world. In the cell the lights are on at day time and night time. The complainant has only got a mattress to sleep on. In the one and half years before in the Maastricht prison Overmaze Q. would also have been kept in isolation, although he was allowed to make phone calls there. The isolation of Q. was extended a few times on base of a letter of the Justice Secretary of State 'about his personality'. 'He is continuously concentrating on possible weak spots in the security system. Also he**

shows an almost pathological interest in materials which could be useful during a attempt to escape', the department writes. The manager mentioned in his written plea that the detainee 'has remained pushing back his frontiers' and 'hasn't submitted to his imprisonment'.
The commission means, however, that B.Q. from his current situation 'has to earn' a human treatment, but that it lacks possibilities for him to do so 'because he is not allowed to have contact with any person and his behaviour is being explained as negative'.
*Source: NRC Handelsblad, 12th November 1993.*

It was a few days before Christmas, when another tormenting took place. Again, a voice behind a helmet visor said: 'Christmas will be good. You're getting sticks on your head!' Brendan thought about it that night. Of course, they could attack him and hit him with sticks. Who was there to know? He told himself he should expect this at some stage. He knew he'd lost weight and wasn't as strong. But fuck it, he wasn't going to let them just do as they wanted without putting up a fight.

His mind was on this when Brendan noticed they had left a plastic knife on the floor. It was just lying near the hatch. To begin with he thought it was a trick to see if he'd take it. That day he just stayed in the cell. When they came to ask if he wanted air, he showed them the small piece of paper with NO on it. That night Brendan moved the plastic knife and hid it. Next day he refused air again. All that day none of them did anything out of the usual. So that evening, he decided he would attack them before they attacked him.

He sharpened the plastic knife till it was like a razor. Next day he would do it. First of all, he would do the team with the riot shields, batons and body armour. They didn't realise in this situation the shields and helmets would work against them.

Brendan waited in his cell for them to call in if he needed air. In his hand he already had the paper with 'YES' ready to show. It was mid morning when they came. 'You know the routine, Brendan' the screw said after he'd shown his answer. He stood up and went to the back of the cell. The knife was in his hand, hidden from view. Taking off the overalls he threw them on the floor and put his hands on the wall, fingers apart and legs apart. Just like he'd practised in the hours before, Brendan hid the knife by pushing it against the wall with one finger. The knife stayed out of sight behind his finger, hand and wrist. 'Okay, he's clean' the team leader said to his team. Brendan turned around. 'Walk slowly towards me' the man said and Brendan did. He had the knife in his right hand by his side. He would take the team leader first, then get stuck into the rest. He knew he'd be beaten eventually but fuck it, he didn't care anymore.

The cell was getting opened. The team leader stepped back to the side, revealing his riot clad team. Brendan knew they would close in around him once he was a few steps away from the cell door. Careful not to make eye contact with the team leader he said, reaching over with his right hand, holding the knife: 'You left this in my cell yesterday'. It was the first time Brendan had spoken in months.

Obviously surprised he looked to the innocent looking knife, which rested on the palm of Brendan's hand. He reached his left hand over to take it. Quick as a flash Brendan grabbed his wrist and twisted it clockwise, raising him on his toes. He then put the knife to his throat and growled in his ear: 'This will go straight through your throat and severe your windpipe, if you move'. The LBB squad didn't know what to do. They knew they'd better keep a distance. He then said: 'What is this about sticks on my fucking head at Christmas, you bollocks?!' The team leader couldn't talk quick enough. He seemed dead scared. The team had all put their batons down and Brendan could hear the alarm siren going off. He knew everything was being caught on camera. 'No one will touch you with sticks on the head' the team leader stammered panicking. Then he said to his team: 'Who said this?'. No one, it seemed. 'If you hit my head with sticks everybody in this room will have retaliation on it, understand?' Brendan said. 'Yes, I do' said the team leader. 'Put your hand out' said Brendan. The man did what was asked. Brendan placed the knife in his hand and gave him a little pat on his face, saying: 'Don't fuck around with me!'

They asked him to return to his cell and Brendan obeyed. Outside the cell door he could hear lots of people come and go, whispering and so on. He thought that any second they would try to jump him in his cell. At this stage he didn't give a fuck about them doing anything.

About an hour later he was surprised by the hatch opening. The team leader said: 'Brendan, may I speak with you?' Brendan nodded for him to speak. He said: 'I never imagined how quick you could have hurt me and how much damage you could have done, but I promise you nobody is going to hurt you here'. He asked what else was wrong in Demersluis. Brendan told him about the food and just all other bollocks: no letters, no phone. 'It's going on too long' he said, 'I know some of my family will be doing things to find out what was going on with me.'

'I'm sorry you are treated like this' the man said. 'I'm just doing my job.'

'Listen', Brendan said. 'You treat people like animals and then get frightened when they turn into one? Just leave. Go on! Fuck off! I don't need to listen to your small-minded opinions on things which are directly your responsibility. You are the one who's leading these idiots!'

Meanwhile the governor ran up, waving his hands and shouting things in Dutch. Brendan watched him through the hatch. He was losing it. Brendan didn't know and had no interest in what Evil Elbers was shouting about. He just said: 'Hey! Enough! Shut the fuck up and fuck off, you fat ugly swine!'

He saw a little smile on the team leader's face when he heard this.

Next day Brendan actually had a hot meal and some fruit, for the first time in months. It was the team leader who was behind it.

He said he didn't agree with the treatment Brendan had been receiving. Later they made a training video of the incident for the LBB squad.

## Chapter Nineteen: Fuel Crisis

Living without any contact from the outside world, without your loved ones, is hard. It's probably the hardest aspect of life in prison. In his cell Brendan looked back at his past many times. The memories of times that his family were still together, especially when he was young, kept him going. They were not well off in those days, but life was sweet nevertheless.

Dublin was crazy back then. It was a great city and there were so many things to do, not to forget the rest of Ireland too. Each Friday they'd go out and get a car. Sometimes Brendan took his dog with him. He would growl when they passed a Garda car. It was funny to see. Brendan had that dog for fourteen years and he understood everything Brendan said to him. He was the best guard dog and was very protective of the house. So much so that the milkman and postman had to leave anything next door. He wouldn't let them in the garden!

A couple of times before this, he had bitten a piece off the postman. Next morning the Garda arrived to shoot him. They came in force. There were a dozen armed Garda, just to shoot a dog. 'Really don't know where he is' Brendan fooled them. 'Probably gone for a walk'. The dog had gone to his uncle's farm for a week.

Brendan was sixteen years old when he decided to go away down to Kerry for a few days with his brother and their friend Mic. They stole a Datsun 260Z sports car and parked it in Dundrum in advance of the trip.

The next day, the government announced that fuel was to be rationed. Ireland tried to shake off the yoke of the British economy, stepped up to the European Monetary System, but saw the value of the Irish pound collapse. It was crisis time.

The three youngsters decided to go anyway and queued up at a petrol station for hours to get the car full before heading off. They stopped in Limerick for the night, booking into a hotel in the city. They had some dinner and went for a walk, ending up in a pub. Brendan left them both half an hour later to park up the car for the night and go to bed.

Next morning, he showered and went up to the next floor for the other two. Mic opened the door. When he went in and looked round the room Brendan could see it was just wrecked. All the furniture was broken and in big carved letters on the wardrobes doors was written 'MIC WAS HERE' and other bollocks like that. Mic was two years older than Brendan. He could've at least carved the wrong name on the fucking doors.

Brendan looked at Mic. He looked nuts. He was just going to say 'let's leave' when the maid walked in. She stopped in the middle of the room and put her hand to her mouth. Mic said: 'Howya ye doing?' to the maid. She smiled and said: 'What in the name of Jesus happened, boys?'

The lads paid her £200 - all they had - to give them a twenty-minute start before she called the manager about the state of the room. So they left Limerick without any money. They'd only been driving for fifteen minutes or so before they realised they needed petrol for the car.

In a small village they found a petrol pump. A sign read 'LOCALS ONLY' due to the petrol shortage. The lads pulled in anyway. A big huge man came out of the office. 'You'll get no petrol here', he said sternly. 'We are practically out of fuel', Mic said from behind the wheel. 'If we pay you £20 for just £10 of fuel, are you willing to help us?'

The man was thinking. 'I'll give you £5 of petrol for the price of £10.'

'Well, give us £10 of petrol and we'll pay you £30'.

'Deal', the man said. Mic handed the keys out to him and the man started to put the petrol in.

Mic was gifted with the blarney. He was talking away with the man, who handed the keys back with a smile. 'If you come back in a few days, we can make a deal again', the man winked. Mic handed him a biscuit saying 'Thanks!' and pulled off. The look on the fellow's face was disbelief. Ye's fucken jackeens!' he shouted. 'Come back!'

Mic thought it would be fun to do as he was told. He pulled in up the road for the man to catch up. They were all laughing so much, their jaws ached. Just as the giant caught up, Mic would pull off again. Mic was laughing so much; he stalled the car. The three of them sharp stopped laughing when the giant threw himself on the back of the car. Mic gunned the engine and shot off. The giant disappeared into the background. 'What kind of an idiot are you, Mic?!' Tony had grumbled. 'The size of that fellow, he would have eaten the fucking car with us in it.' Mic just started laughing, which in turn set the others off again.

They eventually arrived in a village on the outskirts of Kerry and decided to sleep in the car overnight. The next morning, they'd get some fuel. The car was a great car, but it drank the petrol.

After an uncomfortable night in the car, they headed into the village centre in search for petrol. It was early and raining and nothing was open. They found a petrol pump outside a house come shop, just on the pathway.
Mic being Mic pulled up at the petrol pump and honked the horn a few times. There was no response. He got out of the car and banged on the door. Above was the sound of a sash window being opened. An old country man with a night hat like a big tea cosy looked out the top window of the house. He looked like that fellow Scrooge.

Mic said in his poshest accent 'Awfully sorry to wake you, Sir. But we have to get back to Dublin. There has been an accident with my father'. Mic came up with so much nonsense to get him out of bed into the rain, that the man interrupted him, out of pure despondency. 'Alright! Alright! I'll come down' he said, while the sash window closed with a bang. The man gave the lads £15 of petrol for £30. He too was left with a biscuit, peering in astonishment from under the tea cosy as the lads sped off into the distance laughing uncontrollably.

They didn't just use cars for joy riding. The local armed robbery gangs all seemed to own horses. They would be very angry when anyone robbed their horses to ride around. It wasn't uncommon for someone to be found with both legs broken after being caught riding the horses.

Because Brendan and his brother knew all the locals, they heard when the 'vigilantes' would be out all night, waiting for the horse thieves. On these nights, they wisely stayed in bed. When they were not out, the lads were.

On many a night Brendan would get up at 4.00 a.m, get dressed and head to one of his mates in the next street up. Because he could never wake, this mate used to leave a piece of string, tied to his big toe, and hung it out of the window.

Brendan only had to pull the string to wake him up. After he climbed out of the window, they went up the fields and robbed the two fastest horses. They rode them for a couple of hours in the dark, through the fields, before letting them go and going home to bed. They did this for two years, till they grew out of it. No one ever knew who it was. Sorry Noel...

# Chapter Twenty: Pioneer In Vught

The three cars swept in through the gates and up to the reception. Brendan had arrived in Nieuw Vosseveld, the prison in Vught. As his hood was taken off he blinked a few times to adjust to the bright lights. There were over a dozen screws standing around. They stepped back as a tall screw approached. 'Well, well. So, you are Mister Quinn. Wow… I expected you to be six-foot-tall and shoulders out here' the screw said in a jest. As he looked over his shoulder to his men, a smirk appeared on his face. The screws laughed obediently at the great sense of humour of their boss.

Brendan didn't answer, but somehow this screw seemed inoffensive in his manner. 'Bring him to the unit' he said. With handcuffs still on he expected to be brought straight to his cell, but instead they led him to a van with blacked out windows. He was ordered to sit in the back. The doors were closed and the motor was started. As the van started to move Brendan had no idea what was going on.

The ride took about fifteen minutes, but they went nowhere. All the time the van just drove in small circles. They wanted to disorientate him, and it worked. He left the vehicle totally confused and didn't know where the entrance was for a good two months.

He was led into the building, through a few doors and gates and onto a small unit with four cells on it. They stopped outside a cell door. On the way in Brendan had seen a reflection of himself in a window. He'd looked mad. Long hair, a beard, skinny – he looked like a deranged old fool. In the months that had passed he'd been forbidden to cut his hair or have a razor to shave with. He'd also lost a lot of weight. He was 14 stone when they'd captured him, now he was 9.5 stone. His appetite had been affected when they were abusing his food in the Bijlmerbajes. It made Brendan feel angry, very angry. He just had to channel that anger into a sly escape.

The tall senior screw said he had to explain a rule. 'Mr. Quinn, if any screw is taken hostage, the doors will electronically lock and you will be locked in with the hostage. We will then send in a special team to rescue the hostage' he rattled monotonously. Brendan nodded his head in the direction of the cell door and asked: 'Is that my cell?' 'Yes' he answered. 'Open the door. I'm going to bed. And don't explain all that shit to me. Tell it to my future hostages!'

Brendan went into the cell. He was mentally and physically tired and that night he slept around the clock. In the morning he opened his eyes to have a look at his new cell. Table, chair, wardrobe, toilet, sink and even a proper prison bed instead of a mattress thrown on the floor. He hated moving to a new prison. Every time he had to get used to the new faces of the screws. He was hungry and above all he wanted to get rid of the mad beard and long hair. It was time to see the attitude of the screws.

Brendan gave the door a few kicks. Ten seconds after he pressed the 'call button'. The tall screw who was in charge of the others answered. 'Did you sleep well, mister Quinn?' He had the same manner as before. He seemed a lot brighter than the usual oddballs who work in such places. 'Is it alright if we talk?' he went on. 'I will have to explain the rules to you'.

'No problem' Brendan answered. 'But first I want a haircut, a shower and a bite to eat. Only then am I willing to listen to you'.

The screw arranged what he wanted almost straight away. They strapped him into a straitjacket and brought him to the barber. He was allowed to wash himself and finally they served him some food. An hour or so later Brendan was sitting in a cell with a table and some chairs, listening to this screw. He was explaining the rules and stuff.

Brendan was to be one of the first occupants of this special secured emergency prison in Vught. It was called the Dutch Alcatraz. This temporary fortress was the answer of the Dutch government to the series of violent escapes from the four EBIs, which had recently been shut down.

All maximum security prisoners in the Netherlands were moved to Vught, to the 33 cells of the so called temporary extra secured prison (TEBI). The renovated main building of Nieuw Vosseveld was used since August 1993 as the first national super-bunker. At the same time the eventual EBI was being built. This brand new and hypermodern EBI with a capacity of 24 cells would be opened in 1997.

**'In the 33 TEBI-cells lives a horrible company of men. After his conviction, Martin H. moved from the Amsterdam Bijlmerbajes to Vught. The former policeman got twenty years for the murders of mafia boss Klaas Bruinsma and the drug dealer Tony Hijzelendoorn. Besides the drugs traffickers Koos R. and Johan V., alias De Hakkelaar, also the feared Frenkie P, leader of the Venlo gang, was staying in the TEBI. The caravan camper from Limburg is convicted to life imprisonment, with the explicit restriction that he never again will be released into society. One of the gang members of Octopus – Cees H., alias Puck – is staying in Vught, after he blew up a part of the Bijlmerbajes with a semtex bomb in an attempt to escape. Another prominent guest is Brendan Q., who in 1992 took hostages after an unsuccessful robbery on the C1000 supermarket in Northern Amsterdam. Also, Karel P. (the murderer of an orchid grower from Rijswijk), Daniël S. (suspected of the Oklahoma bomb-attack) and drug baron Jakobus L. (alias Kobus the Gipsy) live in a scanty cell in the TEBI-complex.'**
*Source: De Telegraaf, Saturday 25th May 1996*

The TEBI had wings of four cells. Only two prisoners out of the four prisoners on each wing were allowed in the recreation room. They could make one eight-minute phone call a week. This consisted of being handcuffed backwards onto a metal ring which was fixed into the wall. They placed earphones on your head and a microphone in front of you. Two screws or more were always standing beside you during the phone call.

The only people Brendan could use the phone to speak to in the outside world was his mother, sister and his girlfriend. He couldn't speak to any males, like his father, brothers or relatives. He couldn't mention cars, roads or addresses or he'd be cut off.

Of all prisoners in Vught there were only three who never had their hands loose whenever the cell door was to be opened. Brendan was one of them. If he left his cell, he had to stand with his back to the cell door and stick his hands backwards through the hatch in the door. One screw put the cuffs on. Only when the second screw had double clicked it and checked it, was the door opened.

The conversation with the tall screw was interrupted by the deputy governor of the unit. He came in and sat opposite Brendan, looking at him, leaning back in his chair. The others were silent, waiting for him to speak. He wore plain clothes, no uniform. He had glasses and a moustache. He dressed terribly. The whole appearance seemed to Brendan to look something between Groucho Marx and a failed bus conductor.

'I'm Mr. Schotman, the head of EBI.' The prominent stopped and gave it some time to see what impact it had. He cleared his throat and waffled something about his fine officers and his great jail. It was obvious immediately that he and Brendan weren't on the same wave length. He let him finish and dismiss himself with a sway of his coat through the door.

After a few seconds the senior screw asked Brendan what he thought of the governor. In truth, he'd found this Schotman a scary, effeminate character. In Brendan's eyes he was a nasty fairy; he couldn't think of another nickname for him. 'They say you can't judge the book by the cover' he said to the senior screw, who grinned back, nodding.

Vught EBI. What a dump it was. There was nothing to do in Vught that was worthwhile. There was no access to education facilities or any courses, but Brendan continued doing keep fit and yoga. The yoga in particular was great for relaxing. Even Christmas was just another day in Vught. They got an extra boiled egg and a piece of mouldy cake.

The windows of the cell were almost blackened by frosted glass. It was hard to see if it was day or night. Before the frosted glass was a sheet of plastic, then thick pieces of glass in metal squares (like in cop cells), then bars, chicken wire and the sheet of dark frosted glass. Where the air came in from little holes through a ventilator, they blackened it from the outside with a sponge and a large metal clamp keeping it against the holes. If a cigarette lighter was held by the holes where the air came in, it wouldn't even flicker a slight bit, so natural air and light was denied. Also, the windows of the recreation room were blackened out from the outside. In affect prisoners could never even get a glimpse of the outside world from Vught EBI.

The only spot where a piece of the sky was visible was through the wire mesh in the roof of the air cage.

The whole of Vught EBI was security mad. Just to get to the air cage (three separate cages) in the middle of the buildings, prisoners were handcuffed before leaving the cell. Once outside the cell, two screws were present to hand search, slowly and tediously.

The air cage was equipped with 'helicopter security' (wires in which the rotor would get entangled) and 'climb security' (iron bars with 'teeth'). Two screws brought the prisoners, one by one, to the air cage. They only had the key of the prisoner's cell with them, so that they could never open any other door in case of a surprise attack. If a prisoner would take someone hostage, there would be a central alarm from the reception desk and all doors would lock automatically.

Twice a week the prisoners were inspected. The screws called it the 'body search'. This meant that you were brought to an empty cell, where you had to put your hands through the hatch. After the handcuffs were taken off you had to strip and bend down, showing your arse at the hatch. If you refused to cooperate, they would take you to an isolation cell and force you to do it. These visitations took place as standard as soon as you left the wing or came back, except if you had been out for air. Of course, this had nothing to do with security. It was just meant to humiliate the prisoner, nothing else.

Also, when a prisoner had visitors, they were forced to strip, both before and after the visit. Although the visitors always remained behind thick glass. It was completely impossible to have physical contact or pass anything through and although everything was taped in audio and video, they said the inspections were necessary.

All of Brendan's visits were under these conditions. They also drove visitors in the van with the blacked-out windows. Then they were led through some doors where they were strip searched in a room. The management always said they encouraged family contact, but their actions were in complete contrast. Brendan refused to put his family through this humiliation and didn't invite them anymore.

Every prisoner in the TEBI had to work one hour a day. Each morning two prisoners were sat at a table in the windowless recreation room and clipped plastic squares together for plugs. The other two prisoners had to do the same work in the afternoon. The other of the two daily hours outside the cell was spent in the air cage.

Every second or third night two could go to the recreation room, which was a small, dark room with an air powered gym. There was a punching bag, a bike running machine, a rower, a dip and pull up bar, but the equipment was only in use once, maybe twice a week for thirty to forty minutes. The screws watched from an office with bullet proof glass and a reinforced door. Outside this door was a wall of window glass, so they could see prisoners at all times.

To make sure they didn't have to miss a second of action, they also had cameras placed in the ceilings.

The screws were getting more and more annoying. They kept giving misinformation on the silliest things, such as the weather. If Brendan asked whether air time would be in the morning or in the evening, they just gave the wrong answer. Or they said that the post had arrived, while in reality no single letter had come in. It was their methods to make life hell for the inmates. Although no one in this prison could move an inch without being watched, it seemed necessary to constantly provoke the men. The work for instance was so full of drudgery and belittling, it was like an insult, like all kind of childish rules they annoyed them with.

They weren't allowed to have anything else in the cell but only two clothes changes and a plastic comb. Six or seven times a day they searched Brendan's cell. If you wanted to brush your teeth, you had to press the bell and wait for a screw. Waiting could take an hour or even more. Sometimes you got no reaction at all. If you were lucky the hatch was opened by a screw who would give you a toothbrush and paste and wait till you were finished.

At night the cells were checked every half hour. Every single time in the middle of the night the doors were slammed by these screws, who wore hobnail boots to just be noisy and keep everyone awake. All complaints on this were turned away by the so-called complaints committee. This group was supposed to be an independent body set up for prisoner's rights, but these rights didn't seem to exist in the TEBI. They were locked in their cells 21 to 22 hours a day. Food was put through the hatch in the door.

Unsurprisingly there was a lot of tension in the TEBI between the screws and prisoners. Like the other three prisoners on Brendan's unit he hated the screws. The main reason was that they became personal. They did the meanest things. There was for instance a black prisoner in one of the units, who was in bad health. He had been shot in the stomach and used a bag to drain off his bowels. One night he rang the bell and asked the screw for some toilet paper. The screw came back, gave him one square of toilet paper through his night hatch and walked away laughing.

Sometimes Brendan tried to look through the screws eyes to see how they see. All he could put it down to was that they were taking their frustration and problems out on the inmates. They were careful not to attract any attention to themselves. They always passed the buck with a standard reaction, like 'I'm just doing as I'm told'.

It was close to Christmas when he went for a breath of fresh air in the cage. Because it was impossible to have a look outside, Brendan only knew it had been snowing when he entered the cage. He noticed the pigeons that hung round the jail had nothing to eat, so the next time he went out to the cage he took the middle of the bread from dinner with him, which he'd kept for the birds. It was a funny moment when he got the body search and the screws found the piece of bread in his pocket. 'Just hungry' Brendan told them. The screws looked to each other like he was completely mad.

When he got to the cage, he broke the bread up and pushed it through the cage wire. At that moment, the nasty fairy came off one of the units and walked by. Their relationship as governor and prisoner had deteriorated because of the sheer shit this person was making up as he went along. He was a man Brendan had seen make more enemies by his attitude than any other. There were some quite powerful prisoners in the units in Vught. Some were millionaires with lots of contacts and here was this Mickey Mouse, deputy governor of a jail, treating them like sub-humans.

Also, on the heaviest moments in life these screws didn't show any respect or compassion. One prisoner had managed to get permission for a special visit to his mother, who was terminally ill. She had cancer and only weeks to live. He was allowed to say his last goodbye to his mum, but only under certain restrictions. He was only allowed to shake her hand twice: at the beginning and at the end of the visit. The poor fellow had no choice but to agree to the conditions.

At the start of the visit he shook his mother's hand. The screws were behind a screen with shields and batons, just in case the prisoner became violent on the visit with his frail terminally ill mother. It's hard to believe there was so little compassion. At the end of the visit the prisoner leaned over the table and gave his old mother a hug. For this, the visit was abruptly stopped and the prisoner was brought to the isolation wing for two weeks.

Most people with the power to make such a decision, out of pure decency would allow a private last moment with two people, a son and mother. Yet this Mr. governor had the power to be miserable and he took it with both hands, even when it disgusted one or two screws who worked there. You might call these screws sympathisers, who are genuinely decent and who can tell right from wrong. Admitedly, none of the prisoners in the TEBI were angels, but what did this governor win by directly punishing their families? It was hard for Brendan not to hate this man who would take pleasure from two people's most private and delicate moment.

**'Secretary of State Kosto (Justice) is planning to create special crack troops to guard maximum security prisoner in the extra secured prison. He however faces problems in recruiting them.**
**These guards have to comply with high physical and psychological requirements. Only one out of five candidates who are applying is fit to work there. Due to the requested 'extra spirit' the work force will get an intensive education. The Secretary of State has admitted that the temporary extra secured prison (TEBI) in Vught struggles with a shortage of employees. Only 18 of the 33 cells are in use. 'People show a certain reserve to work there', Kosto yesterday declared to the Parliament, which**

**is very concerned about the shortage of work force.'**
*Source: De Telegraaf, donderdag 4th November 1993.*

The pigeons approached the bread. Schotman was watching. He wore black shoes, black slacks and a black overcoat with a red scarf. As his eyes met Brendan's briefly, he timidly looked. Schotman never held a look for long. He left. Brendan watched him go, thinking: Yeah, go home to your family. Get your Christmas tree ready and make it all nice and warm. But before you go, make sure everybody in the unit is as uncomfortable as can be.

Brendan wasn't really surprised later that evening when one of the older screws passed him through an order from the nasty fairy. He had to go out with a dust pan and brush and sweep up all the bread he'd put out for the pigeons. He could imagine Schotman saying it. He was a complete and utter bastard.

Brendan had been in Vught almost a year. Every day he was locked up for 22 hours. If he refused to join the stupid fiddly work on these plastic clips, what they called work, he would stay even 23 hours behind the door. He tried to hold on to the daily physical and mental exercises. Especially yoga, which Brendan had learned from the monks in Ireland, was very important to get through this dead-end struggle.

It was tough: 23 hours a day in a small cell with hardly any way to see out of your window and without fresh air. It would be tolerable if it was only for a short period, but the thought that he wouldn't get out of that blind cell this summer, nor next summer, nor the summer after that and so on, was unbearable. It just seemed too hard to take in that they would keep him there for years and years, torture him psychologically and abuse his rights.

**'When I'm talking to guards, they aim that the detainees are being treated in an inhuman way. A few days or weeks in the TEBI might be bearable, but people who are locked in a longer period never get out the same as they were. In my experience I have seen various clients leaving the TEBI completely prison-crazy.'**
*Source: lawyer Mr. Abraham Moszkowicz in De Telegraaf, Saturday 25th May 1996.*

Again, there was only one way to get a throw of the yoke: an escape. By now Brendan had studied the building well enough. The management and the screws thought this prison was watertight, but there were two ways to break out. Both had 85% to 95% success rates. He had to disappear. One way or the other.

## Chapter Twenty One: The Man With The Red Eyes

It was time to start looking for a partner who he thought was alright. Brendan knew 98% of the prisoners in this Vught super EBI would escape if there was a chance, but who could he rely on? Who could keep his mouth shut about his preparations?

He managed to set up a communication line with Husnu, the Turk with whom he'd been staying in the prisons of Sittard and Hoogeveen. He knew he was in Vught on another unit but they were completely isolated from each other. At least, that's what the work force in the TEBI assumed. In reality they talked to each other by using stubs of hand-rolled cigarettes. During their earlier imprisonments they'd developed their own alphabet. Before air time, in his cell, Brendan wrote a message to Husnu on the inside of a cigarette paper. He rolled the cigarette, went to the cage, smoked it halfway and shot it in the corner. When it was Husnu's time to get fresh air, he picked up the roll-up, unrolled it and read the message. After that he shot his own prepared cigarette in the corner.

Eventually the screws discovered it. They brought the stubs to the TEBI-manager Paul Koehorst, who started to study the evidence, but couldn't read it. He even sent the stubs to the United States, where experts had to crack the code. It was all in vain. Their alphabet was only accessible to them.

Brendan had to find someone else to cooperate with. Most of the prisoners in TEBI were foreigners. One of them was Armando, a Colombian of 51 years of age. He was the co-defendant of Ruben Londoño, with whom Brendan had escaped from De Geerhorst in Sittard. Armando was a very proud man with a lot of dignity. Brendan decided to approach him.

For the first few days, the times they did see each other during air time, they never spoke. Brendan thought he just wanted to be left alone. It suited him. Four or five days later Armando and Brendan were called to the recreation room. It was evening. Armando was sitting with a chess board in front of him. Brendan was watching the English news.
'You want to play a game of chess?' he asked. Brendan looked at him. This was 'the man with the red eyes' as he was called. This nickname was quite unequivocal; Armando had bloodshot eyes. Life had deeply furrowed his face. 'Sure', he said. 'Let's set up the pieces'. Settling himself behind the board he put his hand out. 'My name is Brendan'. The two men shook hands. 'I know who you are. Everyone here does. I know some people who speak very well of you' he said. Brendan waited for him to continue, but he didn't. He presumed he meant Ruben and another fellow who was helping with the Sittard escape.

Armando was doing 14.5 years for the very same crime Ruben was convicted for: the smuggling of 2,658 kilograms of pure coke with a street value of more than £75,000,000 in 1990.

He'd been unfortunate from the start with the deal in Holland. He was already going home, after he had sold his quota and turned his back on the coke business. Ruben however offered him a lot of money to stay and help. With regret he went with Ruben to a restaurant, where they would meet two men. Ruben told Armando to sit at another table and keep his hand in his jacket, like he was carrying a gun. Armando also had to keep looking at the table Ruben was sitting at. The two men had kept glancing over at him. 'It was very risky' Armando had told Brendan. 'I asked Ruben: What if they pull guns out and shoot me first, thinking I'm the danger? That evening in the restaurant our fate was sealed. It was the night Ruben refused to give the extra £25,000 for 'extra protection', because he already had paid. I heard Ruben call: 'Greedy sons of bitches! You've had enough!' If Ruben would have paid, none of us would have been jailed'.

It's easy to figure things out looking back, Brendan thought. His life would have been quite different if he could've seen his mistakes in advance. After the record catch of drugs, the ministry of Justice placed Armando and Ruben in the EBI-circuit because of the threat of a liberation attempt by the Colombian coke cartel. The four captured Colombians were of great strategic value for the syndicate.

The fear of Justice wasn't without foundation. Quite soon escape and liberation attempts were flying in Holland. On New Year's Eve 1990 the first Colombian was taken out of the prison in Arnhem by using a revolver and a rope ladder. Less than a month later four men tried to liberate Ruben from the same prison in Arnhem. With aluminium collapsible ladders they climbed over the wall and reached Ruben's cell. After forcing the window bars by use of a cutting torch, they tried to smash in the bullet proof window with a sledgehammer. The action took too long. The liberators left just in time, without Ruben. One year later, in January 1992, Ruben escaped eventually – together with Brendan from De Geerhorst.

Also, Armando had already broken out once. On 30 March 1993 he escaped from De Schie in Rotterdam, only seven months after Brendan broke out of there. Armando succeeded to bribe two screws and smuggle in a fire arm. Together with a 45-year-old American he took hostages and walked out of De Schie. The two escapers didn't get far. The assistants who had to bring them to the other side of the river by boat, didn't show up. Armando stopped a learner car, threatened the instructor and his student and tore off. In the city the two bumped into a lamppost. Armando got out of the car, but was arrested shortly after in the centre of Rotterdam. He got twenty months on top of his punishment. Also, his advanced release – the deduction of a third of the punishment – was taken away from him.

Brendan got on well with Armando. They had respect for each other and after Brendan sat down they had a good game of chess. Armando was a smart player.

Over the next few months, they spent more time together on recreation and in the cage. That was possible thanks to another inmate, who was put on their wing and stayed in his cell for 24 hours a day. He was an informer of Justice, and he knew that Brendan knew. He didn't dare to come out of his cell, so the others took his recreation time.

Armando was easy going and well educated. He had an academic degree in psychology. He considered the system of the Vught TEBI a violation of human rights. The Colombian started to teach Brendan Spanish, mainly so they could talk more freely in front of the screws. It took a few months but Brendan picked it up and soon they were mostly speaking in Spanish.

One day a screw called Armando over to the glass door. The screw simply said: 'Have you got a sixteen year old daughter in Colombia, called so and so?'
'Yes, I do' Armando answered. 'Well, she's dead. She had an accident and slipped in the bath' the screw informed him as cold as ice, after which he retired to the office.
Armando walked over to Brendan and sat down. He knew Brendan had heard what this screw had told him. 'Did I hear that pig correctly?' was the only thing he said. Brendan could only nod yes. He could see the disbelief and heartbreak in his eyes. He didn't know what to say. What can you say to someone in a situation like that? He looked over at the screws in the office. They had also been told and were looking over very smug. Brendan looked away and put his head back looking at the ceiling. He tried to give Armando some kind of privacy for that moment.
'Maybe it's a mistake' he heard Armando say in Spanish.

Brendan had heard and seen enough now. He walked over to the door and waved the screw to come. 'Set up a family phone call for Armando now! I'm warning you; don't fuck about it!' he commanded.
The screw realised this was not the moment to be obstructive. He went back in the office and made a call. He came out and said: 'Twenty minutes.' Brendan nodded. Armando made his call.

Brendan waited for Armando to come back. His face and body language said it all: it was true. Armando was devastated. Only one week earlier he was talking about her, saying how she was doing so well in school and other things a father would be proud of. His face was impassive, but his eyes were like a window to his despair.

The way the screw had told Armando was so very cold, very crude. Just like he was saying dinner is ready. No compassion; it was typical of them. Armando went through this sad time with a lot of dignity. Brendan couldn't imagine how he must have been feeling in his cell at night.

It was around a month later when the same screw came into the recreation room to tell Armando more bad news. His wife had had a heart attack at home and had passed away. Brendan's blood ran cold when the screw said it again with the same contempt as before.

Armando was just alone in the world. He had lost his youngest daughter and his wife. Family dying is every prisoner's nightmare, especially when you're in such a place like Vught TEBI, in a tiny little cell on the other side of the world.

Brendan would never forget the pleasure the screw took in telling Armando the bad news. But Armando was strong. It's truly amazing what your mind can deal with, but things like that take their toll on you. Armando bent, but didn't break.

In 1996 Armando was transferred to a regular prison wing with a lower security level. Sometimes in prison you meet people who you miss once they're gone. Armando was one of them. He always remained a gentleman and Brendan missed his company, but was glad he was on his way out of Vught. The lawsuit due to his failed escape from De Schie in Rotterdam was finished. He got two years extra.

After a while Armando wrote Brendan a letter from De Geerhorst in Sittard. He had stayed a while in Maastricht under normal regime. Eventually he would end up in Vught again. The reason being a new liberation attempt in De Geerhorst. In the morning of 18th September 1997 a helicopter appeared above the air yard of the Sittard prison. As one of the rotors hit a lamppost the chopper crashed. The pilot died in the flames. According to Justice the action was meant to release Armando. He had been the only one who ran over the courtyard as the helicopter was hanging above it. Armando suffered burns from the crash.

Three and a half years later, on 19th February 2001, Armando was released. From his cell in Vught he was transported immediately to Schiphol airport. Guarded by two members of the military police he was flown to Bogotá.

# Chapter Twenty Two: The Promise

Because he couldn't see through the window what the weather was like, Brendan asked a screw about it one morning. He said: 'It's a nice sunny morning out there.' He turned his back to the door hatch to get himself hand-cuffed. He was in his shorts and T-shirt and looking forward to a run for an hour.

They opened the cell door and with two screws right behind he went through the few doors down to the exercise yard. As they went through the last double doors, Brendan saw it was raining cats and dogs. He turned to one of the screws and said: 'You told me it wasn't raining!' The screw shrugged and said 'Must have just started'.

'Bring me back to my cell!' he snarled. 'You know the rules' the screw said. 'Once you leave the cell, you must complete the air time!' The second screw pushed him in the back and almost tripped him up. Brendan turned around and the screw pushed his face against his and said: 'Walk!'.

He made Brendan's blood boil and he pulled the handcuffs half way up his backside and at the same time bent down and pulled his arms up. The anger gave him so much power, that he forced the handcuffs to break in two.

The tough men suddenly shrank into two runty guys. 'Brendan, don't hurt us. We're sorry. We didn't mean to hurt you!' they suddenly sounded.

Brendan looked at them and wanted to just let loose on the one who pushed him. Instead he just said: 'Don't ever fucking take advantage of me again!'

The screws asked if he would please pretend to be handcuffed and go back to his cell. Brendan just replied: 'Shut the fuck up and open the fucking doors on the way back.'

Breaking handcuffs was something he did a few times. Every single time the screws got scared to death when he suddenly showed them his hands. The only screw Brendan talked to was Jopie Jansen, the head screw on this unit. Jopie was six feet tall and had a grey ponytail. He was a philosopher and quite popular with the detainees. Jopie knew Brendan could break the cuffs. He'd watched as Brendan had sat down opposite him, cracked the shackles and sat with folded arms. While the two screws behind grew rigid with fear, Jopie smiled and offered him a cigarette. 'Brendan', he said at the end of the talk, 'don't scare anyone, put your arms on your back and walk back to your cell'.

Quite soon after the incident with the lying screws the nasty fairy was ranting at how the handcuffs could be broken. They never said anything to Brendan about it, but that very same week TEBI-manager Paul Koehorst (appendix 4) gave an order to change all handcuffs into new heavy steel handcuffs.

There was a lot of intimidation in Vught. The screws made the life of some prisoners a misery. It was completely over the top with security. Every time the prisoners found a way to get out of some rule or other, they came up with a new one. They were being heavily oppressed.

Sometimes in these places it was too much for a person to take. The attitude of the screws, the sleepless nights due to the cell checks, the air vent going all night and the stamping of the heavy metal capped boots of the night patrol; some of the prisoners simply broke and ended up seeing doctors or psychiatrists. They begged for sleeping pills and nerve pills. Brendan would never condemn a prisoner for going like that. People are just different. But he would never speak to anyone involved with the jail. They talk shit. Besides that, you never knew whether or not they treated your innermost feelings discretely. No one could guarantee that your information wasn't passed on to the screws.

Twelve prisoners, including Brendan, brought their lawyers together to make a court case against the rules and conditions of the prison. Brendan's lawyer was Mr. Jos Coumans (appendix 5) of the Van Asperen office in Maastricht. He was sharp and he was getting sharper by the day. Brendan had full confidence in him and Van Asperen.

The subjects the lawyers presented in the court case were the lack of natural air and daylight in the cell, the confinements of 22 to 23 hours a day, the skin-searches and the hold back of visitors and post.

The lawyers managed to have a crew from the national TV-programme Nova getting access to the prison. The Ministry of Justice allowed them to interview prisoners. The screws put it around that there would be a 'payback' down the line for any prisoner cooperating with Nova. Brendan couldn't care about them making things difficult. He was going to say what he thought was right.

Eventually it turned out only Brendan and a Dutchman called Fred would do it. In front of the camera he drew up a list of abuses that occurred in the TEBI, like prisoners being kicked up in the isolation unit by the fucking screws. But once on television, Nova seemed to be pro-Vught. They hardly brought up the things Brendan pointed at.

The judge dismissed most of the complaints, but they won one important thing. Once a month they could have a family visit without the glass screen in between. Brendan was pleased with that. Finally, he could see his family again. The shameful reception and searches were finished.

**'The regime in the temporary extra secured prison (TEBI) in Vught will not be changed. There is no matter of separation of detainees and the regime is not in contravention of article 3 of the European Treaty of Human Rights.**
**That is determined yesterday morning by the President of the Court in The Hague, Mr. A.H. van Delden. The summary proceedings were started by thirteen detainees in the TEBI.**
**Van Delden says the regime in the TEBI in itself is not in contravention of the rules of conduct as alleged by the plaintiffs.**
**Nevertheless, he thinks the regime can't bear the test of criticism on two parts. Those are the arrangements concerning the visits of the next of kin and making phone calls to their lawyer.'**

***Source: De Telegraaf, Wednesday 12th January 1994.***

But when Brendan asked for an application form for a family visit, he was told that the new rules didn't apply to him. Somewhat confused he got in touch with his lawyer who assured him it was his right to have visits without having to be in a bulletproof terrarium.

The management of the TEBI stuck to the denial. He would abuse the new rules by trying to escape, they reasoned. Well yes, they were correct to say that; Brendan was already making plans to have a helicopter fly in.

The escape would take only two and a half minutes. He would leave at night. The advantage of a break out during night time is that no one expects it. Furthermore, the operation had to take place in the air. Fleeing by car would cost extra minutes.

The plan was as follows: when the helicopter had appeared above the exercise yard, two well trained men would quickly jump out. On their backs they would carry a sledgehammer with a long handle, plastic explosives and guns. The chopper would leave immediately. With the hammer they could slam the electric locks off of the first, second and third couple of automatic doors. Having reached the office, where all keys were hanging nicely numbered on the wall, thirty to forty seconds would have gone by. With the explosives they would blow out the window, climb inside, grab the keys of the unit and the cells, open the office from the inside and get Brendan out of his cell. After that they could run the same way back to the exercise yard. After one and a half minutes the helicopter would appear again to pick them up.

With a heavy heart Brendan cancelled the attempt. He'd made a promise to a girl he'd had met a year before in London, after his escape from the Pentonville prison. She insisted that he stay in and finish his time. She had endured two of his escapes already and had to live with a man that was always on the run or behind bars. He didn't want to put the relationship at stake. She meant a lot to him.

The bottom line was the Dutch didn't believe him. They thought Brendan was still planning to escape. In one sense he was so much more relaxed that he wasn't paying much attention to the screws. They were using all the energy, not him. But in the other sense, no more escapes, he couldn't get over it for a long time. It was one of the times in Brendan's life he really found hard. Like he was letting them win. Usually he'd be waiting to have the last laugh by escaping. Being in jail is bad, but when you know you're not escaping, the time drags by 3 times slower.

Sometimes in his cell at night he seriously tried to talk himself into breaking the promise and go. It was a difficult choice. He was in his thirties; young and confident of any help he needed outside. He would have loved to escape from Vught. The screws and the management really thought it was escape proof. Brendan had to genuinely struggle with himself to just stay and be a prisoner year in year out.

**'In the EBI in Vught I noticed for the first time a declining psychological development in Brendan's mind. Prison life had started to gnaw at him. There were moments he had enough of it. He neglected himself, his condition. One day he even wanted to be extradited to Ireland or the United Kingdom. 'It might be hard there, but at least it's fair', he said. I found that a remarkable development.'**
*Source: Mr. Jos Couman's former lawyer of Brendan Quinn, September 2004.*

Brendan was going to the shower through the usual tedious security. He'd had his hands cuffed through the hatch in the door and a body search by some new screws. Suddenly he'd had enough of it. He objected. 'All I've got on is a pair of shorts and a towel over my shoulder. Stop all this nonsense and take me to the shower.' he demanded. The little Surinam screw answered with a short yell: 'No!'.

Brendan was standing with his back to the door, hands cuffed behind his back. This little screw went to put his hands out to stop Brendan from moving. As soon as his hands touched Brendan's chest, in a flash, he kicked his feet from beneath him. The screw went down on the floor, hitting his elbow. He jumped up and ran at Brendan, pushing. Brendan went to side step, but his flip flop caught the lip on the cell doorway. He felt himself falling back, still cuffed, without his hands free. He fell back onto the bed, hitting his arm. The door slammed shut and locked.

Safely the other side of a locked door now, the screw opened the small hatch. While he was looking in, Brendan summoned all his strength to break the new type of handcuffs, but they wouldn't. Going over to the door he shouted: 'I will make you pay for that!'. The screw wasn't impressed 'First opportunity I have', he said, 'I'm putting you on report'. Brendan slowly and calmly said again: 'You will pay dearly for this.'

Next morning, Brendan was called out of his cell for a visit. Thinking it was his lawyer, he put his hands through to be cuffed and went out. Along both ends of the hallway were a dozen riot clad screws. The nasty fairy was coming to punish him over his little pig screw. Brendan was actually looking forward to this. It would give him the opportunity to pay him back double. The prison boss had just moved into a new house he had built. A sympathetic screw or a double agent screw had given Brendan the address. At the time he wasn't sure if it was a set up, or if the screw was alright. 'The only thing I want', the screw had told him, 'is that Schotman will be beaten up in his own house'.

Personally, Brendan had no interest in this. He ignored jail people like governors and screws, unless they got personal with him. He took the address anyway though. You never know when something like that could come in handy.

The type of punishment the boss had in mind for Brendan due to the incident, was one fine piece of management skill: two weeks isolation.
Just before he was brought to the cell, Brendan saw a chance to strike back. Looking him in the eyes, he leaned over and whispered his new address to him. The reaction was funny to see and Brendan could see the fear in his eyes. He had been waiting to have a go. Now he just looked like the idiot he was. Brendan knew he'd gagged him and was quite satisfied with that. While he was in the isolation cell, the boss would now be worrying himself sick at how Brendan had got the address.

He lost count how many times he was thrown in the isolation cell. In the years that had gone by he'd got used to the fact that it happened without any reason. Inside the isolation cell it was clinically clean. Except for a green plastic airbag and a bible, there was absolutely nothing in it. The airbag was meant for you to sit on, but this was simply impossible. Within half a minute you slipped off it. The walls were bright green and the dark frosted glass in the window made any views outside useless. The radiator was built into the wall and gave off a sickly horrible heat. The cell door had wire glass panels in it. A big solid steel door closed over the cell door to seal it.

Brendan was only allowed overalls and socks, nothing else. In the morning he was allowed to wash and walk around for half an hour in the concrete air cage with bars on the ceiling. The rest of the day nothing happened, except for 9 p.m. At that time a mattress was thrown into the cell for the night. All meals were delivered through the hatch in the door.

Each time the steel door was opened for air or the mattress he was ordered to take off his overalls. He then had to stand naked while they handcuffed his hands behind his back through the hatch in the door. Once cuffed, they would open the door, come in and start the search under his arms, in his hair, mouth and ears. Then he had to bend down so they could look up his arse. After that Brendan had to show them the soles of his feet, one by one.

This strip search was twice a day, fourteen times a week, not including the three or more unexpected searches. There was no logic in anything they did. Brendan never left his cell except for half an hour air, so with the best will in the world he was never going to be able to smuggle something into his cell. These visits were just meant to humiliate. There were always six or seven screws doing the searches.

**'Holland has been reprimanded yesterday because of the regime in the heaviest secured prison of this country, the EBI in Vught. According to a sentence of the European Court for Human Rights detainees are being treated 'inhumanely and degradingly'.**
*Source: De Telegraaf, Wednesday 5th February 2003.*

From being in these poxy little cells for years Brendan's eye sight had got worse. He went to the optician, which was basically the empty cell opposite, which they used for strips searches and the doctor.

The expert didn't agree with Brendan that his eyes had adapted to the poor natural light and short distances, all those years in these cells. 'No, no', he said, 'it's not a problem'. He did some tests and prescribed new lenses. If he had a headache, he said, he could swallow a paracetamol. It looked like the doctor in Vught was secretly working for the paracetamol company, because all the years he had been there that was all he ever did. For any condition: two paracetamol tablets. Brendan thanked God that he'd never needed any serious medical help in there.

# Chapter Twenty Three: Sick Of Holland

Brendan had had enough of the Dutch prison system, especially Vught and had asked the Irish embassy in The Hague to start extradition proceedings. Although he knew he was hated in Ireland, he wanted to serve the rest of the sentence in his home country. In Ireland he would be able to have visits from his family and friends in a respectable way.

He was dying to embrace them. Especially for his parents the many years imprisonment, and also Tony's, were like hell. They didn't deserve a terrible life like that. Brendan's parents were the most decent people you can meet. Thanks to them, Brendan had a wonderful childhood. Both hard working and law abiding, they made sure their children went to the best schools available.

Education was always a serious affair. Brendan went to a college run by brothers. They were like monks, dressed in habits and he really couldn't remember seeing any of them ever smile. They had two punishments which they would dish out for the least of reasons. He lost count of the number of times he'd fallen foul of the cane. Six of the best across the tips of your fingers on a winter's day was no funny thing.

Brendan was a studious, hard working schoolboy. Each year he would get the best marks in every exam. Most of all though, he liked the sports and in particular karate. He took it up in a club in town, run by two brothers, staying with them for around three years.

Both Brendan's parents came from big families but with very different backgrounds. His mother came from Firhouse, a posh part of Dublin, whereas his father hailed from Fatima Mansion, one of the roughest estates in Dublin.

As kids, Brendan and his brother grew up in one of the most notorious estates in Dublin. There were different little gangs, mostly specialising in armed robberies. There were a lot of republican families too, mostly IRA, but some INLA. It seemed that once you got older, there was a high probability you would either go into crime gangs or republican gangs. It was hard to get legitimate work in Dublin in those days.

Brendan tried nearly everywhere, looking for a part time job after school. He'd walk for miles, asking in almost any type of business he saw, but nobody seemed interested in hiring a young lad of twelve or thirteen years old. Nevertheless, it was carefree days, in those long summers and short winters.

The estate was like most big estates, except for the calibre of the people. The Garda were hated by nearly everyone in the area. If anyone was ever found to be speaking to them, local people would deal with them severely. It was an estate that didn't tolerate informers. They would be rooted out. The Garda would only come into the estate in force.

Brendan had just turned fourteen when his father became ill with agoraphobia; fear of open spaces. He'd never heard of it before but it can strike anyone anytime. Some people don't leave the house for twenty years with it.

Brendan's father suffered for five. After around a year of his dad staying in, money started to become less and less. Things started to become too expensive and the house started to go downhill.

Brendan and his two brothers were too young to get jobs and even a part time job had proved too hard to get. Weekends at home were becoming hard. His dad sent Brendan over to his aunt Maura's to lend ten Irish pounds. He was doing this and going over nearly every Friday. Brendan didn't like it but he always did as I was asked to do.

He felt upset about his dad being unwell and no money being in the house every weekend. One day it had upset him enough that he decided to do something about it. When Friday came and he was asked to go to his aunty Maura for a £10 note again, Brendan just decided to go out and get it himself. Asking his brother to come with him they set off. Brendan said: 'I'm going to get some money. I don't know where, but I'm not going back to Maura again!' His brother agreed.

They walked the few miles into Rathfarnham, a posh part of Dublin. At a big shopping centre they watched while a couple parked their car and went to the shops. Brendan went over, opened the door, pulled the wire under the wheel and hot wired the car. The car started, he picked his brother up at the entrance and drove off. They then went to Dundrum shopping centre, parked up and went in. Having filled up a trolley to the brim with food they just walked out, put the stuff into the car and drove off again. This time they went to the gypsy camp and sold the car for £200. They got a lift home with the shopping and Brendan told his brother not to say anything about it.

At home they told their parents they'd found a wallet with £180 in it. They said there was more in it but they'd gone shopping. Brendan's parents were only concerned if there was an address in the wallet to send it to the owner. 'No' he lied, 'it only had money in it'. If they'd known the truth, they would have been very angry.

'Next week we both have a job' the lads told their parents. 'Every Thursday and Friday evening we have to work at a club, cleaning up and helping stack drinks and so. We'll each earn £35 an evening with it.' Their parents were delighted, the lads were working and staying out of trouble. Brendan felt guilty lying to them, but he'd rather that than have no money and have to visit one of his relatives every Friday to lend money. Fuck that!

In fact, there were no obstacles in the way of an extradition to Ireland. Brendan's court cases were over. Of the twenty years that were sentenced, he won back four on his appeals.

He had a visit from the Irish embassy, who assured Brendan his application to go back would be dealt with specially. He was told that they'dd heard about his case and felt he'd had a bad deal with the length of his sentence and the conditions he'd been kept in.

'I tried to visit you before, when you were in isolation in Demersluis' the diplomat

told Brendan. 'I went back to The Hague, after the prison management told me you refused to talk to anyone from the Irish embassy'.
'That's complete nonsense' he told him. 'No one ever told me you have tried to visit me.' It didn't surprise him. Brendan knew they did things like that all the time. The diplomat promised to visit again soon.

Some time later the embassy informed him that an extradition to Ireland would be out of the question for some time. The United Kingdom would be on top of the list. The British hadn't forgotten that Brendan still had to serve his time after the escape from Pentonville prison in London. But at that stage he couldn't really care where he ended up. All he wanted to do is leave Holland so he said 'yes' to England. Procedures started, but Brendan would remain on high security for years. The Justice department still considered him a merciless criminal, who was constantly after an escape. They didn't trust him an inch.

**'I herewith inform you that:**
**Based on the consideration that, in view of your detention record, you still represent an extremely large security risk; that on numerous occasions you have escaped using hostages and/or brute force; even during your detention in the TEBI you have demonstrated an extreme interest in the security system and you have also attempted to try it.**
**Based on your behaviour during your detention in the TEBI, namely un-predictable behaviour, that your attitude represents a continuous threat to the staff which you maintain in a variety of ways. You also assume an extremely dominant role in the department.**
**There are uncertainties concerning your possible extradition to England, concerning which you indicate that should the extradition not take place you will have nothing left to lose and the true Quinn will manifest himself.**
**Based on the above I deem it impossible to suspend your handcuff regime at this time, that this would involve unacceptable risks in reference to proper order, peace and security.**
**In February 1996 your case will once again be discussed by the Selectie Advies Commissie (Selection Recommendation Committee). After this meeting I will once again review the measure concerning the handcuff regime.'**
*Source: letter from the director of the penitentiary institution Nieuw Vosseveld in Vught to Brendan Quinn, 16th August 1995.*

Brendan had supposedly lost all his credits. All these screws were say-ing he showed no remorse and rubbish like that. Who do you show remorse to in jail? In his mind he heard the judges pronounce the judgements: twenty years in total, including his punishment in Ireland. The punishments they'd imposed on him were outrageous by Dutch standards. The escapes had clearly played a role in the determination of the sentences, as well as the media attention on the C1000 robbery. With his escapes Brendan had embarrassed the prison system and they just did everything they could to make him pay for that.

A screw who was sympathetic to him had once told him the whole of the Dutch system was on his shoulder and he and his colleagues were told to break him. They tried to, indeed, but none of the many petty measures they used against Brendan had any effect. He was unbreakable due to the fact that only one thought kept him busy: escaping. Also, the hate he had for what was happening to him kept his energy level high all the time he was in jail. Only the period in which Brendan had pushed every thought of an escape from his mind, because of the promise he had made, was unbearable. The days seemed so much longer. Everything was double the effort.

His life in prison didn't make any sense. Stuck in a vicious circle. He'd already had escaped three times from jail, and three times he'd been arrested again. Most of the years in prison had been spent in isolation. Year after year, locked in a tiny cell for 23 hours, without daylight or fresh air. Just to think about it made Brendan angry, but all things considered he was the one who had made the mess and nobody else. He would just have to deal with it.

Brendan never blamed anybody else for his convictions. It was his choice to commit crimes, so he was the only one to blame. It was he who took the risk of being shot or spend years behind bars. Now it was time to look to the future. Within a couple of years, he would have to work and lead a normal life. Yes, he'd be one of the unconcerned people he'd been watching in shopping queues, without having the fear of suddenly being captured by a special squad.

The general thought that a criminal gets to repent in prison, is non-sense. The harder the regime, the more frustrated, obstructive and damaged prisoners become when they come back into society. Except for the fact that criminals are taken off the street for some time, society doesn't gain any advantage from it. It's hard to explain what a number of years in jail does do to you. It for sure doesn't do any good. Being in prison doesn't change your criminal mind. You can only do that yourself. A prison just introduces people with criminal minds to each other.

Brendan had met a lot of people in the Dutch system. Most of them only thought and spoke about what they were going to do when they got out. Every time it was the same story: going back into crime. But for Brendan he'd reached the end of the line. He'd been in jail almost half his life now. Through much of his thirties he was locked in on the isolation unit. He'd spent long enough behind these thick cell doors to put his freedom at stake. Crime now was something in the past for him. It had to be.

One morning he was called out to see the barber. As he got out lots of screws were there. Brendan thought the gentlemen of the EBI-management were up to something nice for him once again. And indeed, behind the screws the head of the nasty fairy appeared. 'Bring him to the isolation' he ordered. Brendan had become used to this carry on over the years. He hadn't been told why he was in isolation, although he'd never asked either, suspecting it just had something to do with the move to England.

The isolation dragged into weeks and Brendan was getting pissed off. One day the big door opened and then the hatch on the cell door. Through the glass panels he could see the face of the nasty fairy. He was looking in. 'I have something to say.' the fairy said. Brendan got up and walked over. At that moment he'd have loved to spit right in his face through the hatch after his usual silly few seconds of half smiling to himself.

He said: 'Well Quinn, you have been the worst prisoner in Vught and we had many battles.' Right on that moment Brendan knew he was going to be moved. 'Now listen' he said. 'You've been a fucking arsehole, but it's not personal. You're a jailer, I'm a prisoner.'

'I never thought you were seeing it like that' he said full of surprise. Brendan just shrugged. Behind his back his fists were shut tight. He'd have loved to use them on this horrible coward's face for a few seconds.

'From now on, all your mail will be blocked.' Brendan looked at him and thought: 'You just can't help yourself, can you?' His post had been blocked for years already. All this time he'd spent in Dutch jails, he'd never seen a newspaper. 'Fuck off, you horrible little bastard!' Brendan shouted. He was furious. The fairy started shouting back. The other screws were all watching as the two men called each other all sorts of names. They all worshipped this arsehole and that's why they only worked in the isolation, doing his dirty work.

The nasty fairy shouted that he knew people and could get them after him. Brendan laughed at him and thought how he'd been right all these years. He really did think he was some kind of big shot. Brendan walked away, sat down and ignored him. When the cell door slammed slowly shut that was the last contact he had with the fairy godfather.

That night a screw put his face to the hatch on the door, after Brendan had got onto the mattress. 'I just want to say fair play to you. You always stood up for yourself. Tot ziens!' He didn't answer, just nodded.

He woke the usual time and started the normal morning exercise. It wasn't long after when he heard lots of footsteps. It wasn't normal to hear footsteps at this hour. They were coming towards his cell, at the end of the hall. Suddenly, as the footsteps reached his door, Brendan realised they had come to move him away.

They went through the search procedure and escorted him to the unit entrance. The doors were opened and he was brought to the van with the blacked-out windows, which drove to the entrance of the jail. Once there they were met by the members of the special transport unit BOT. Some faces he hadn't seen before. The hood was put on and Brendan was put into the second of the three escort cars. Members of the squad got in either side of him. These two guys tried to intimidate him with a gun. One of them slotted a bullet into the chamber beside Brendan's hooded head.

These rides through the country were most annoying, especially because of the crap drivers. Quite a few times Brendan had thought the car would crash. This time the motion of the moving car was making him feel sick. After all these years in a poxy cell this car was alien to him. He started to puke. One of the squad members pulled the hood up and put a plastic cup under his mouth.

Eventually the car stopped, they'd arrived at their destination. Brendan heard the sound of aircraft. The hood was removed and he was walked to the steps of the plane. As he reached the top of the stairs, he looked back at the semi circle of armed men with their guns on show. It was as if they were saying: 'Get away and never come back'. They did have a right to feel that way, he thought. He was the intruder.

On the plane the Dutch handcuffs were taken off and the British ones put on. Brendan was astonished to see there were only three English screws around. He sat on the inside seat. 'What's this all about, with this police army around?', one of the screws asked.
'Just a mistake of the Dutch Ministry of Justice' he answered. 'They confused me with another fellow named Quinn who also was in Vught. He's what you call a real criminal!' The screw just nodded.

The plane started to move. After a few seconds Brendan felt the plane leave the Dutch tarmac. 'Finally!' he thought, overjoyed about turning his back on Holland. Down on the ground, he thought, some of the people were thinking the same.

## Chapter Twenty Four: Looking Back

It seems most appropriate to let Brendan have the last word:

'They say if you have no regrets in life then you haven't lived properly. Looking back over the years I do have a few regrets.

Top of the list would be having put my parents through so much worry. They deserve so much better.

Also, to anyone who crossed paths with me in my former line of business. It was nothing personal and I hope you all understand that and that there are no hard feelings.

I spent years in the most notorious secure units in Holland and England. The abuse and injustice I experienced from the horrible cunts who hide in screws uniforms would torment any decent man, but what's done is done.

Today I'm just a normal law-abiding citizen.'

# Appendix One

*'I was staring death in the face'*
*'Wim de Boer, former manager C1000 supermarket*

The worst thing someone can say to Wim de Boer is that 'it will pass by. Because it won't' the then manager of the C1000 says, thirteen years after the robbery and hostage taking in his supermarket. 'After a while you realise that you're not able to shut it off. It comes back every now and then.'

For three hours De Boer – 37 years of age at that time – felt the barrel of Quinn's gun in his neck. During the lengthy conversations about the dramatic event, the amiable supermarket entrepreneur sometimes has to observe a moment's silence. He doesn't fight the tears. If they come, they come.

'At the time itself, it didn't really affect me that much. I knew they were coming for the money, not to shoot me. The supermarket had to be supplied and these guys were wasting my time; this is how I experienced it, the first minutes of the robbery. I am rather commonsensical; a gift from my mother. Looking back this character trait probably saved my life. When I heard afterwards what a highly dangerous type of criminal this Quinn really was, I realised that I went through the eye of the needle. I had stared death in the face.'

'During this hostage taking I was incredibly aware of the fact that I shouldn't irritate this Quinn. Be friends, stay relaxed; that's what I thought all the time. I think this was my salvation in the end. By using my brains, I took care to stay alive. For instance, after a while I said to Quinn in all soberness: 'Well, how about a cup of coffee and a snack? You guys can have a drink. The beer is on the house'. Quinn had to laugh about it. By this the atmosphere became less tense.'

'Actually, it's ridiculous that I remained so relaxed. Probably this attitude contributed to the fact that this hostage taking – how strange it may sound – was concluded in a quite decent way. No single slap was given, no voice was raised. Nevertheless, I found it extremely humiliating how our people had to lie down on the floor, with their chest on the floor and their hands on their head. It was like what you see from Guantanamo Bay. The very same happened to us. John the grocer was incredibly scared. 'Will we survive this, Wim?' he asked me. 'Yes, we will. Stay calm, everything will be alright' I answered.'

'Once we were at the safe, I offered Quinn this wallet with 10,000 guilders. 'Are these banknotes marked?' Quinn asked. 'Of course' I answered in all honesty. He had to laugh on that one. 'It's shit-money' he said. When Quinn started to hand out money to the employees, the mood changed a little. That was of great importance for the situation.'

'Quinn was sensitive to sentiment. When we talked, I told him a personal story about every employee. This way everyone got an identity to him.

He was willing to release someone once in a while. Thanks to my character I managed to influence Quinn and win the battle'.

**'The men were thinking to quickly seize half a million guilders on the first working day after Easter. Supermarket manager Wim de Boer however made clear that the safe wouldn't automatically open before half past eight. He could only hand the men the special 'robbery wallet' with 10,000 guilders in it. According to judge Mr. S. Slagter the drama came to a good ending thanks to the admiring courage and self control of Wim de Boer.'**
*Source: De Telegraaf, 18th August 1992.*

As the hostages were released and the three criminals surrendered, De Boer got a little giggly about the way the police approached them. 'Although the robbers had already had thrown their guns away and were lying, isolated on the ground with their hands on their neck, an army of armed squad members with bullet proof screens crept up on them very strategically. At that moment I thought to myself: how about me? I had a gun against my neck for three hours. Did I have a protection screen?'

'After the tragedy everyone hugged me. 'Thank you for saving my life', they cheered. Only then I realised that they could have been right.
Outside more than a thousand people were applauding for me. The whole scene had been live on national television. My heart was fit to burst at that moment. I hadn't foreseen the impact of the hostage taking.'

Commonsensical as he is, De Boer reopened his store the very same day. He visited his wife who was in hospital recuperating from a serious disease, went to the police station to get interrogated and was overrun by all kind of social workers. About twelve hours after the incident De Boer collapsed. 'I'll never forget it: the RTL4 news bulletin of 7.30 p.m. started with the topic. I could handle it without problems, until the moment pictures were shown on TV of the robbery on the Albert Heijn supermarket in Oosterbeek, two years earlier. This drama cost two lives and a serious casualty. That was the moment I broke down completely. I had to cry like hell. Just in a split second I had realised that my life had gone through such a tiny hole. I cracked up completely. Everything hurt. All I felt was pain. A hammering heart, sweating, cramps. It was all one physical discharge of emotions. At once you see how close you have been to death. Fortunately, I didn't realise that during the hostage taking'.

The memories always come back, mostly unexpected. 'In a movie, when hostages are taken, I have to turn my head and look away. Some time ago an employee of mine walked through the supermarket with the hood of his tracksuit on. In a flash I saw Quinn. I was scared stiff, got goose bumps. I explained this to this innocent boy and asked him to never wear this hood again. A short time ago a supermarket of a colleague of mine was raided. He was shaken by it and had problems to restart again. I looked him up and went out with him for one day. We just drove around the country, had a chat about minor things and did some work in his supermarket. With my experience I was able to help him and distract him a little. But after this day I was struck by a terrible headache! I had kind of absorbed all the tension'.

Recently De Boer delivered a lecture about the raid in front of a class of police students in Amsterdam. One of the students was his son. 'I talked about it for one and a half hours. It was quiet as a mouse and very emotional, also for my son and his fellow students. I had talked about the incident to my son before, but when I went as deep about it as I did in this classroom, he saw for the first time what it had really done to his father.'

'Looking back, I can say this drama didn't break me. On the contrary, I have grown mentally by it. I find that hard to say, because it will look like I want the whole world to know about it. On this April day in 1992 I learned to know myself. I was subjected to a severe test and I did stand it. When I'm facing a difficult challenge nowadays, I'm having a great confidence in a good ending. I dare to take more, because I know it will be fine after all. During a vacation in the sunny south, my wife and I looked each other in the eyes and said to each other: nothing can happen to us anymore.'

# Appendix Two

*'I just improvised a way out'*
*Gerard de Wit, police-negotiator during the raid on C1000*

'Brendan Quinn? He was a dirty bastard!' Gerard de Wit, the then police sergeant who negotiated with Brendan Quinn during the hostage taking in the C1000, remembers the Irishman like it was yesterday. Moreover, the events have had a strong impact on his later life. De Wit – t-shirt, jeans, tattoos on both forearms – has left the force by now and lives on the Caribbean island Aruba.

'Quinn took his hostages in a dirty way. I told him during the negotiations that he was a terrible coward to take women for hostage', De Wit says in broad Amsterdam, thirteen years after the raid. 'Apparently, he took notice of that, because quite soon he released a girl and a woman.'

'I remember he was running in and out constantly to negotiate. He carried a Browning FN 9mm. As I saw that piece, I thought: you have to be a very good shot to hit me with that. In the meantime, he continuously pointed the Browning to the head of the manager. Quinn insisted that I would bring him my boss. 'He doesn't speak English' I bluffed immediately. Looking back, I have to laugh about that. I promised him all kinds of things, but I constantly tried to make clear to him that he wouldn't get away anyway. To promise and give nothing is comfort to a fool, I once read in an American book about negotiating techniques. I didn't know a thing about tactics. I just improvised a way out. What did I know? Before I joined the police, I was on the ocean-going trade. I was just a sailor in a police suit.'

'As Quinn came out with the manager, having the gun to the man's skull, I thought: If he pulls the trigger, the hostage will fall and this criminal will be a sieve the very same moment. I estimated that he also had figured that out already and decided not to give in an inch. In the years after I thought many times of that decision, which I took in a split second. I took a risk and perhaps that was a wrong thing to do. It was out of the question that these people would get away. They were desperados. If they had fled into the city or the province, the consequences would be devastating.'

'My wife Gré Vasse – she has died in the meantime – was a senior police officer at that time at the police station at the Waddenweg. In a big conference hall, she took care of the victims with coffee, cake and heard their stories. It was a disaster. Everybody cried. I watched the victims as well. They were broken down, defeated. How logical can things be. Having a gun on your head, early in the morning! A bastard like that doesn't sense what impact that has on a human being.'

'I found it heavy as well. After the incident I was completely empty. I laid three days on the couch, unable to do anything. To me the raid on the C1000 was the last drop that made the cup run over after a series of shootings.

For one and a half year I was in therapy due to a post traumatic stress syndrome with Dr. Gersons, who now is Professor of Psychiatry in the Academic Medical Centre (AMC) in Amsterdam. There I started to realise that I only worked on sixty percent of my capacities. They went to the bottom to sort everything out in the AMC, but fortunately I came out like I was born again.'

# Appendix Three

*'Nobody was like Quinn'*
*Joop Elbers, former governor of Demersluis, Bijlmerbajes*

Joop Elbers, the then governor of Demersluis, characterises Brendan Quinn as 'the most control-problematic detainee' he has ever met in his long career. About twelve years after the ways of the prison-governor and the criminal parted, Elbers (62) is for security reasons willing to answer questions about his experiences with Quinn only by a chat-session on the internet.

*Mister Elbers, is it correct that Brendan Quinn was detained in Demersluis under your charge?*

'That is correct. In 1992 Brendan Quinn was offered to me by the ministry of Justice'.

*What did you know about Quinn at that moment?*

'I knew Quinn was a very dangerous criminal. During his escape from De Schie, together with Mohammed M., it proved how dangerous this man was. Also, the desperado-like behaviour appeared during the raid on the C1000-supermarket in the north of Amsterdam. Everyone in the Netherlands could witness this live on television. Together with Mohammed M. Quinn can be considered to have been the trendsetter of the series of hostage takings that overran the prison system since then.'

*What effect did the crimes of Quinn have on the prison system?*

'Until the moment Quinn and M. committed their very violent escape from De Schie and traumatised different prison employees, the Netherlands had a very human prison regime. Only after their escape was copied many times, structural security measures were taken. The initiative wasn't specifically taken by the prison system.'

*Especially for the detention of Quinn the complete isolation unit on the top floor of Demersluis would have been cleared. Is this correct and what was the reason for this initiative?*

'This is correct. After exhaustive consideration and study, it seemed that the situation on pavilion 4A – the house of detention for control-problematic detainees – still provided too much danger to place a detainee of this calibre. No other institution was qualified for taking Quinn at that moment. For that reason, it was chosen to place Quinn in a cell on the roof pavilion and have him guarded by a

LBB-team; a special patrol group of six people with helmets, long batons and shields. At that time Quinn was the only occupant of this isolation floor. It was a compromise of the ministry, until the moment a definitive alternative would appear for the detention of Quinn'.

'The reason for clearing the top floor for Quinn was that he was a continuous danger for his environment and extremely dangerous involving escaping. Quinn constantly sensed for opportunities to break out and he actually made attempts to do so. He is the most control-problematic detainee I have ever met in my career.'

'Quinn stayed two periods in Demersluis. After the first months he was ex-changed with Mohammed M., who was detained on the national separation unit in Maastricht and with whom Quinn had escaped from De Schie. In Maastricht Quinn was more comfortable than he was in Demersluis and that was the purpose. But he went misbehaving again and had to be put in a punishment cell several times.'

'After five months in Maastricht, in which he became more and more difficult to approach, he was brought to the Rode Pannen in Veenhuizen, in consideration with the ministry. Over there he was very tense and explosive. Quite soon the tension got so high, that he kicked through the security window of a cell. These windows are prepared for a lot of violence. This incident demonstrates that the man was as strong as an ox and that he could be, using his body as a deadly weapon to all those who stood in his way.'

'Quinn got fourteen days in a punishment cell and was sent back to Demerslu-is. Because of his behaviour he was back to zero again. With the ministry we decided to put him in a punishment cell, until the moment he was placed in the TEBI in Vught definitively. On 9 November 1993, after about twelve weeks in the punishment cell in Demersluis, Quinn was transported to Vught.'

*What made Quinn so threatening to you?*

'In prison Quinn set up conversations with guards and let them easily tell where they were living. He filed this information in his brains. Even after four years he knew in details what this guard had told him and what his address was. Prison guards can take a lot, but when one of the prisoners suddenly tells where they live, they collapse. The fact that he knew made him so threatening. I have seen many horrifying people, but nobody was like Quinn.'

'The daily report of the LBB-squad showed clearly that he kept resisting against detention. He did that by keeping his body in shape on a very active way, by training extensively. Of course, this isn't prohibited and he wasn't to blame for it, but the fact remained that he was extremely strong. On his fingertips he did his press-ups, hour after hour. All the time he was sensing, moving. Quinn was a sportsman on a top level. He was like Schwarzenegger, but only more, much more supple. Those muscles were developed so extremely, one wouldn't wish to come in between.'

'Quinn also kept threatening the squad members of the LBB. He did that during his whole stay in Demersluis. He kept pushing back frontiers to sense the reactions. With his attitude he inspired fear in the guards. They were always tense when Quinn was out of his cell.'

'Although Mohammed M. escaped three times from an EBI and from Pavilion J of Maastricht, and although he took high risks with that and caused damage to prison employees, he was only half as dangerous as Quinn, experts and experienced employees claimed. I share this opinion. Quinn had nothing, really nothing to lose. I believed his threats. If he said he wished me dead, I believed it as well. When he left Demersluis, he left a note that he would have me assassinated in my own house. I believed that he would have me killed as soon as he got the chance.'

*What made you decide to have steel plates welded together at the walls of Quinn's cell?*

'I took that decision because Quinn almost broke out. The contractor who built this prison made everything out of concrete, except for the outside walls – these were made out of bricks. To Quinn bricks meant nothing; he dislodged them easily. He got them out with a toothbrush. Mister Quinn was already getting the window frame out. He had the plan to kick out the wall, climb into the cradle of the window-cleaners and get down in it. After the cell was altered, Quinn finally had no reply. He was captured like a bird in a cage.'

*Quinn states he was treated like an animal in Demersluis and was kept much too long in isolation. What is your view on this?*

'If Quinn says we turned him into an animal, I say: you only come in this place when you have behaved like an animal. I never have had the wish to hurt Quinn, but he was a special case that had to be approached on a special way. We always have tried to do that within the bounds of the law. If we really would have wanted to keep him silent, other scenarios would have been thinkable. Quinn has stayed in the heaviest secured prisons. Now he is out, he of course has a big mouth. I can't deny however what he claims in this book.'

'To keep someone in isolation for such a long period is out of our view, but in extraordinary cases we don't have a choice. Out of sheer necessity I had to tie him down, to ensure the safety of my employees.'

*Quinn has started several complaint procedures, amongst other things because he had to sleep on a mattress without sheets on the floor.*

'We didn't give Quinn a bed for security reasons. I refused to provide a man of such calibre with things that could be abused against the employees. Because of the same danger Quinn also wasn't given a mattress cover and sheets. It is possible to braid a club or to commit suicide with it.'

*Eventually you were rapped over the knuckles by the complaint committee about the detention of Quinn. His lawyer Mr. Nico Meijering reported a crime against you, involving maltreatment. Also, the state department of criminal investigation started an investigation against your personal role in this matter.*

'I entered an appeal against the verdict of the complaint committee and I won it. The conclusion was: Elbers simply had no other choice with a detainee of this calibre. Everything we did inside the prison was between the bounds of the law. Moreover, I wasn't the only one behind the decision to keep Quinn detained this specific way. It was determined by the ministry of Justice and by experts from the prison system. Eventually I was the one who signed for it and carried the responsibility.'

*Eventually, what would you like to say to Brendan Quinn?*

'If he manages to survive outside the prison walls, I would find that terrific. It would mean it wasn't all for nothing and I'd wish him all the best. However, time will tell if he'll stay on the rails.'

# Appendix Four

*'Quinn was a great psychologist'*
*Paul Koehorst, former general manager of the EBI in Vught*

The fact that Holland created an EBI-superjail in Vught, is a direct consequence of Brendan Quinn's escapes. This is stated by Paul Koehorst, former general manager of prison Nieuw Vosseveld in Vught. Koehorst was one of the main characters behind the creation of the special fortress. 'Quinn forced the Dutch authorities to take absolutely un-Dutch measures.'

For four years Koehorst was the highest host of Brendan Quinn in the TEBI, the temporary extra secured prison. The manager of Quinn's unit, Gerrit Schotman, wasn't willing to look back on his experiences with the Irishman, Koehorst declares. That's why Koehorst himself acts as spokesperson:

'Because I was in charge in Vught, Quinn always wanted to talk to me. I have always refused to get in contact with him. Quinn had his own manager, so he had to talk to him, Schotman. Quinn tried to challenge Schotman constantly. When Schotman walked by with a pile of papers under his arm one day, Quinn called: ' Hey, postman!' Schotman called back: 'Yeah, but a free postman!' Quinn couldn't stand this in the presence of the other prisoners. Quinn always wanted to play the big boss, the central person in the jail. He always wanted to dominate.'

'Quinn was one of the first occupants of the TEBI. All those years he was kept in the special handcuff regime. We had our reasons for that; Quinn tried out all kinds of things. He had a tremendously good nose for people who were nervous. He intimidated and threatened them to the limit. He had respect for people who weren't afraid of him. Brendan Quinn was a great psychologist. I found it regrettable that he was on the 'wrong' side.'

'Quinn looked with a penetrating gaze into the lens of the security cameras. He also showed a special attention for locks, doors and procedures. He made indirect inquiries about the security system and about the private lives of the guards. 'I only have to say the word and they are coming to get me out of here', he said once in a while. The next day he would come back on it: 'You weren't thinking I was joking yesterday, were you?'

'Quinn tried everyone out. The guards had to be careful all the time. If he handed his dirty linen through the hatch of the door, you could bet on it that one piece was lacking. If the warder would be so stupid to bend and ask Quinn about it through the hatch, he would get dirty underpants thrown in his face. Eventually Quinn also contributed to a better and safer TEBI. Thanks to him the prison got better handcuffs. Quinn was so strong; he could break the cuffs. He pulled them under his bottom, used all his powers and ignored the pain he must have felt in his wrists. The handcuffs were not strong enough for Quinn. We had to replace them all. That was a tough job. I remember it took us weeks to find stronger handcuffs.'

'Also, the doors are better secured thanks to Quinn, after an incident with a jail-or. Quinn sent this guard away by telling him some story – the man had to bring him a chessboard or something like that. As the man was walking away, he heard a click behind him. He turned around. In a flash he saw the arm of Quinn disappearing through the hatch of his cell door. Quinn slid the deadlock on the outside of his cell door. After that incident, we added an extra slide on every single door, on an unreachable distance from the hatch.'

'Looking back, I can say that we accomplished our mission. We managed to keep Quinn inside, even without accidents. Brendan Quinn was in the first place a prisoner of his own character. I didn't put him in the TEBI, he did it himself.'

# Appendix Five

*'They were continuously afraid of Brendan'*
*Mr. Jos Coumans, former lawyer of Brendan Quinn:*

'Brendan was a caged beast' says Mr. Jos Coumans, the lawyer who assisted Brendan Quinn for years. 'After a while caged beasts show neurotic behaviour. Brendan didn't. He was always busy, keeping his body and mind in top condition. Brendan was not the body builder type; he was an athlete. He was as strong as a bear. Everyone could see that. This neck of his, it was one piece of strength. It was obvious to everyone that you better shouldn't have an argument with this guy. This is what he radiated, by nature. Everyone was afraid of him. Big or small, broad or thin, he didn't care what type of person he was confronted with. If necessary, he would have a go at anyone.'

'One way or the other it clicked with Brendan. I could get along with him very well, partly because I never passed any moral judgement on what he had done. Brendan started up a series of legal proceedings, about 20, 25 I believe. Of course, I knew that he did this just to be out of the cell for a minute and have a chat.'

'I also could say to him: 'Brendan, with this complaint you are really whining.' He could react like: 'Okay, I assume you're right.' You always needed strong arguments to convince him. There has never been any controversy between us. Brendan put his total confidence in my hands. If I said: 'This is how we do it', he said. 'Okay, let's go for it.'

'The Ministry of Justice was furious after his escapes. The extra secured prisons were a matter of prestige. I also dare to state that the EBI in Vught was directly originated by the escapes of Brendan.'

'Justice tried everything in its power to take away Brendan's right to have an early release. In Holland it's every prisoner's right to get released after having done two-third of his punishment, unless he has misbehaved seriously enough in prison to lose this right to have an early release. In all Brendan would have to do six more years than usual. This intention of the Ministry of Justice came to Brendan like a smash in the face.'

'The lawsuit about taking away Brendan's rights took place in Arnhem. The courthouse's cell block was downstairs. The only person around was an older messenger who didn't care too much about anything. I said to him: 'I'm here to see my client, Mr. Quinn'. The man pointed his finger into the direction of a cell and said: 'There he is. Open the door yourself.' That happened more often; the suspects couldn't get away anyway. Brendan saw me standing there, came out of his cell and looked around. The scales fell from his eyes. 'Jos, are we the only ones around here?' he asked.'

'Down the hall were about three other courthouse' employees standing together. Brendan got very nervous. He even started to shiver. Escaping now could easily cost him three years extra. He was standing there with an attitude like: 'If I knew this in advance, I would have gone already'. We went upstairs, but having arrived there, the case against Brendan appeared to be put off, due to an ill translator. Brendan was brought back to prison again.'

'After a few months the case came up in court again. This time the situation was totally different. Instead of only three courthouse employees, there was an army of heavily armed Berets present. Snipers were lying on the roof. Everyone was body searched and at the cell block there were about nine of these fitness blokes. I wanted to get to Brendan, but these guys didn't go aside. After a lot of discussion, I squeezed myself through the many shoulders to Brendan. He saw all these people standing and said with a sigh: 'Shit!' He realized that only a few months earlier he had the ultimate chance to break out. Eventually everything ended successfully. The demand to take away Brendan's early release was rejected, which meant that Brendan didn't have to do six more years in prison.'

'Brendan was a man of note in jail. He didn't want to be seen as some kind of hero however. Brendan realised that the bigger his name was, the more Great Britain would ask for his extradition.'

'Brendan knew how to use the prison guards for his escapes, without these people noticing it. Among the four or five guards who were in his area all the time, there were always two or three who were somehow touched by Brendan. Brendan was a master at creating a relaxed and informal atmosphere with these guys. Unsuspectingly they were interrogated by him. Brendan told them for instance that he owned a beautiful fast car, with all features on and in it. Then he asked the guards what kind of car they had. 'What? A Citroën? You're joking! You're not going to tell me it's such an ugly red one, are you?' 'No, I've got a yellow one', a warder answered for instance. Brendan filed all this information in his brain. Eventually he knew every single detail about the guards. He realised it could be useful one day.'

'In Maastricht there was a jailor who was boasting about being such a great combat sportsman. Brendan teased him saying that there's nothing like a good street fighter. During this teasing Brendan made up the score. Then he would ask me: 'You see this screw over there, Jos? He's scared to death of me. Watch.' I warned Brendan not to fool around, because he risked an extra few years easily. But Brendan just couldn't help doing it. He was in the door of his cell and gave the guard a hand. On the very same moment Brendan pulled the combat sportsman quick as lightning and with an incredible force into his cell. 'It's a joke man' he laughed, while the deadly scared keeper didn't know how fast he had to leave the cell. 'Did you see that, Jos?' Brendan asked, as he came out of his cell with a broad smile on his face.'

'Combat sportsmen or not, the guards were always too late. His speed and power made Brendan a feared prisoner. No one dared to give him a friendly pat on the shoulder. It cost the people so much energy to guard him. They always had to watch out for him. They were continuously afraid of him. When Brendan for instance was handing back a dinner tray with plate and cutlery, he held it only a short moment longer in his hands than the guard expected. On a moment like that he played a psychological game of just a split second. The guard would be standing stiff scared because something unsuspected could happen. If the tray would fall on the floor, Brendan would run amok again.'

'The lawsuits against prisoners like Brendan, Mohammed M. and Husnu A. always passed with a lot of struggle. These were the merciless criminals, the prosecutors reasoned. But when the case was handled in appeal at the court in The Hague, the atmosphere was totally different. The first emotions of the crime were some kind of cooled off then, but moreover the judges were more down to earth, thinking: it's not hard to understand that these people escape when the prison is full of bent screws.'

'In Vught Brendan wanted to use every single possibility to expose the prison regime. Eventually I brought a case with two other lawyers on behalf of all fourteen TEBI-occupants, in December 1993. The then president of the court in The Hague, Mr. Van Delden, came to Vught himself to have a look. He was a fantastic judge. He wanted to talk to detainees, but their hands and feet were shackled. Van Delden said: 'I'm not going to talk with cuffed prisoners'. He was advised not to do it, but the shackles were taken off. Three prisoners talked to him and it led to an improvement of the regime.'

'In the EBI in Vught I noticed for the first time a declining psychological development on Brendan's mind. Prison life had started to gnaw at him. There were moments he had enough of it. He neglected himself, his condition. One day he even wanted to be extradited to Ireland or the United Kingdom. 'It might be hard there, but at least it's fair' he said. I found that a remarkable development.'

'Eventually Brendan went back to the UK. I received a postcard one day. Brendan Quinn is a remarkable man.'

## Operation Sayers

Operation Sayers takes a detailed look at the notorious Sayers brothers rise to the top of the criminal ladder on the backstreets of Newcastle's West End and the authorities attempts to bring them crashing back to earth by any means necessary.

The Sayers family were once described by 'Northumbria Police as a 'new breed of criminal.' Brought up in the West End of Newcastle by a career criminal father and a mother who was a paid up member of Mensa they were always going to rise to the top of the criminal tree.

The book exposes corruption at the highest level, the use of drug fuelled informants, and how one member of a rival family broke the criminal code to land Stephen Sayers in court. The book also reveals for the first time the full details of 'Operation Insight' which was set up to put Stephen Sayers in jail for the rest of his life.

Available now from www.badboysbooks.net

The Sayers: Tried and Tested At The Highest Level

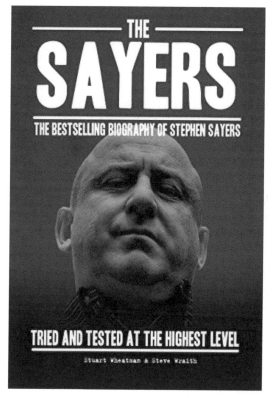

Stephen Sayers is one of the most feared men in the country, with a reputation that's preceded him in the dozens of prisons he's served time.

The Sayers family have been known on the streets of Tyneside for decades. No one else comes close to their level and it is widely known that they 'run Newcastle'. Rumoured to be behind countless violent multi-million pound armed robberies, unsolved gangland murders, extortion rackets and organised crime in general, Stephen, his brothers and associates are an unstoppable force. They've remained tight-lipped about their exploits… until now.

Stephen earned respect at an early age, blazing his own trail and coming out on top by any means necessary. A true bad lad in every sense, he gives us a first-hand account of growing up as a Sayers and living up to the reputation that the name holds.

Available now from www.badboysbooks.net